Thank you for picking up my book. Your support means a lot, and I hope you find the read both enjoyable and insightful. Beyond being an author, my work extends into research and consultancy within organizational behavior and leadership. I engage with a broad spectrum of clients, from individuals to larger teams and organizations, offering guidance in leadership development.

For a deeper dive into my professional background and consulting philosophy, several websites are available. There, you'll also find my contact details. I'm eager to hear your thoughts on the book or discuss potential collaboration in leadership coaching.

Discover more about my work and other publications related to leadership and organizational behavior at my personal website, https://thomaspatrickhuber.com.

Learn about my specific approach to leadership coaching and consulting at https://elevateus.ch, the official website of my company.

Lastly, in case you want to reach out to me directly please send me an email at thomaspatrick@mac.com.

I appreciate your support in purchasing this book and look forward to connecting with you.

Wishing you an enlightening journey,

Thomas P Huber, PhD, MS ECS

Dedication

This book is dedicated to the visionaries, the trailblazers, the pioneers. To those who see beyond the horizon of the present and dare to dream of what lies ahead. It is for the leaders who not only adapt to change but embrace it, shaping the future with their unwavering commitment to innovation and progress.

Your courage to challenge the status quo, your resilience in the face of uncertainty, and your unwavering belief in a better future inspire us all. This book is a tribute to your journey, a celebration of your transformative impact, and an acknowledgment of the paths you have forged for the generations to come.

May your vision continue to light the way, and your actions inspire a legacy of change and excellence.

Foreword

In this book, "Leadership Transformed: Strategies for the Next Generation of Organizational Excellence," we delve deep into the myriad questions that resonate with every contemporary leader, questions that often linger in the quiet hours of the night. At the heart of these inquiries lies a fundamental quest to understand the evolving dynamics of leadership and organizational behavior in a world that is continuously, and sometimes abruptly, changing.

How do leaders stay motivated and keep their teams driven during and after unprecedented crises like a global pandemic? As we navigate through and emerge into a changed world, the answers to these questions become pivotal. This book explores the various work environments - in-person, hybrid, or remote - and examines which of these foster high-performing cultures. The pandemic has irrevocably altered the landscape of our workplaces, and understanding these changes is crucial for any leader aiming for excellence.

Agility has become a buzzword across industries, but its implications run deep. "Leadership Transformed" is a journey into the essence of agility in leadership – how can we be more adaptable, responsive, and resilient regardless of the industry or sector we operate in?

Complex human interactions in the workplace form the crux of organizational dynamics. This book aims to unravel these complexities, providing insights into how leaders can effectively manage and lead diverse, multicultural workforces. The diversity in a team can be its greatest strength if harnessed correctly, and this book provides strategies and perspectives to do just that.

We are at the cusp of a technological revolution, with generative AI and other advanced technologies redefining the scope and approach of leadership. "Leadership Transformed" not only addresses the impact of these technologies on leadership abilities but also explores how leaders can leverage these advancements to enhance decision-making, improve efficiency, and foster innovation.

This book is more than just a collection of theories and ideas; it's a compendium of answers, strategies, and insights drawn from extensive research and real-world experiences. It's designed for leaders who aspire to transform their approach, adapt to the changing world, and leave a lasting impact in their organizations.

As you turn these pages, you will find yourself equipped with the knowledge to tackle some of the most pressing challenges and opportunities in modern leadership and organizational behavior. "Leadership Transformed" is your guide to navigating the complexities of today's (and tomorrow's) leadership landscape.

Introduction

In recent years, the world of leadership has undergone a seismic shift, driven by rapid technological advancements, global economic fluctuations, and unforeseen challenges such as the COVID-19 pandemic. These changes have not only altered the way we conduct business but have also reshaped the very fabric of leadership.

Today's leaders are navigating through an era marked by complexity and uncertainty, where traditional leadership models and strategies are being challenged and redefined. The emergence of global connectivity, the rise of a more socially and environmentally conscious generation, and the relentless pace of innovation demand a new approach to leadership—one that is adaptable, empathetic, and resilient.

This introduction aims to briefly explore the contours of this changing leadership landscape. We will examine the need for new strategies and approaches that can effectively address the complexities of our global, interconnected world. The focus is not just on surviving these changes but on thriving amidst them, leveraging the challenges as opportunities for growth and innovation.

As we proceed, we will dig into how leadership is no longer confined to the upper echelons of corporate hierarchies. It has become a dynamic, inclusive process that resonates at all levels of an organization and beyond. In this new era, leadership is about fostering collaboration, driving change, and inspiring a shared vision amidst a diverse and often dispersed workforce. The integration of advanced technologies, the shifting paradigms of work environments (from traditional office spaces to remote and hybrid models), and the increasing emphasis on social and environmental responsibilities have added new dimensions to the leadership role.

Leaders are now required to be visionaries, capable of anticipating future trends and preparing their organizations to adapt to these changes proactively. They need to be innovators, embracing technology not just as a tool for efficiency but as a catalyst for transformation. And importantly, they need to be connectors, bridging diverse cultures, generations, and geographies to create cohesive and effective teams.

We invite you, the reader, to explore these new realms of leadership. It is a guide for current and aspiring leaders to navigate the challenges and harness the opportunities of this ever-evolving landscape. As we delve deeper into each aspect of modern leadership, our goal is to equip you with the knowledge, strategies, and insights necessary for leading with excellence in the 21st century.

The primary aim of the book is to provide readers with a profound understanding and actionable insights into the realm of effective leadership within contemporary organizational settings. This book is meticulously designed to serve as a compass for those navigating the often turbulent waters of modern-day leadership.

At its core, we seek to bridge the gap between traditional leadership concepts and the demands of today's fast-paced, diverse, and ever-evolving global business environment. The book offers a forward-thinking perspective, acknowledging that the challenges leaders face today are vastly different from those of the past. It provides a roadmap for adapting to these changes, not just to cope but to thrive.

The insights and strategies presented in this book are grounded in a combination of rigorous academic research, real-world case studies, and the latest trends in leadership and organizational behavior. Each chapter is carefully crafted to delve into various aspects of leadership, from motivating teams in a hybrid work setting to leading multicultural workforces and leveraging technological advancements like generative AI.

One of the key objectives of this book is to equip leaders at all levels – whether you are heading a small team or steering a multinational corporation – with the tools and knowledge to lead effectively in their respective domains. It goes beyond mere theoretical discussions, offering practical strategies, examples, and action plans that can be implemented in real-world scenarios.

The book also recognizes the importance of personal growth and continuous learning in leadership. It encourages readers to reflect on their own leadership styles, embrace self-improvement, and develop the resilience and adaptability needed to lead successfully in an ever-changing world. We place a strong emphasis on the human element of leadership. It explores how leaders can foster a culture of inclusivity, empathy, and ethical practice, which are essential for building trust and achieving long-term organizational success.

The purpose of "Leadership Transformed" is to serve as a comprehensive guide for current and future leaders. It aims to inspire a new generation of leadership that is equipped to handle the complexities of modern organizations, drive innovation, and create a positive and lasting impact in their industries and communities. This book is an invitation to embark on a journey of leadership transformation, one that aligns with the values and demands of our times.

To fully grasp the essence of leadership, it's essential to embark on a journey through history and across diverse cultures. Leadership, as a concept and practice, has evolved dramatically over time and varies significantly across different global contexts. The historical evolution of leadership theories presents a fascinating tapestry of changing perceptions and practices. The early 20th century was dominated by the Great Man (Woman) Theory, which suggested that leaders were naturally born, not made, and that leadership was an attribute of a select few. This perspective gradually shifted towards the Trait Theory, which sought to identify specific qualities that characterized effective leaders, such as intelligence and charisma.

As the century progressed, the spotlight turned to Behavioral Theories. These theories proposed that effective leadership was not solely about inherent traits but was more about learned behaviors. Various leadership styles, including Democratic, Laissez-Faire, and Autocratic, emerged, each proposing different approaches to leadership behaviors.

In the late 20th century, Contingency Theories gained traction, advocating that there is no singular best way to lead. These theories, like the Situational Leadership Theory, argued that effective leadership depended on various factors, including the nature of the task, the environment, and the team's needs.

Leadership is a concept that transcends boundaries but is also deeply influenced by cultural contexts. In Western cultures, leadership often emphasizes individualism and democratic principles, in contrast to Eastern approaches, where collective well-being and hierarchical respect might be more ingrained.

In regions like Africa and Latin America, leadership is often intertwined with community and family, with a strong focus on relational and communal leadership. Conversely, in Nordic countries, leadership tends to be more egalitarian and participative. Understanding leadership requires synthesizing these historical and global insights. It becomes clear that leadership is not a static concept; it is dynamic and context-dependent. As societies evolve and cultures intermingle, especially in the age of digital communication and globalization, the demands on leadership also transform.

Effective leadership today is about adaptability and inclusiveness, about understanding the nuances of different cultural backgrounds and historical contexts, and about being responsive to the ever-changing global landscape. This broad perspective sets the stage for a deeper exploration of leadership in contemporary times, highlighting the need for flexible, culturally sensitive, and innovative leadership approaches.

Leadership, fundamentally understood as a dynamic and relational process, transcends the conventional confines of directive management and hierarchical control. This concept emphasizes the importance of interaction, collaboration, and the pursuit of shared objectives, painting leadership not as a static role, but as a journey marked by continuous evolution and change.

At the heart of leadership is its relational nature. It's about forging connections, empathizing with team members, and nurturing a sense of shared purpose. This aspect of leadership elevates it beyond mere task management; it becomes about creating an environment conducive to effective collaboration and collective success. Integral to this relational approach is emotional intelligence – the ability of leaders to understand, empathize, and manage relationships with sensitivity and insight. This creates a culture rooted in trust, respect, and mutual support. The multifaceted dimensions of leadership further extend its scope. It encompasses strategic thinking, where leaders not only envision the future but also chart a practical course towards it. Decision-making is another critical facet, involving choices that align with organizational values and goals. Moreover, leadership involves mentoring and coaching, guiding teams towards both individual and collective growth.

A pivotal aspect of modern leadership is its role in managing diversity and fostering inclusivity. In a globalized world, leaders often work in cross-cultural settings, navigating teams with varied backgrounds and perspectives. Embracing and leveraging this diversity is essential for organizational success and innovation.

Leadership as a relational process is comprehensive, encompassing a range of skills and attributes that go beyond traditional management. It's about relationship-building, strategic visioning, inclusive decision-making, and creating an environment where both individuals and teams can excel. This perspective is key to understanding the dynamics of contemporary organizations and steering them towards success in a constantly evolving landscape.

Effective leadership and followership are underpinned by a combination of essential traits, skills, and attitudes that contribute to the success and health of any organization. These elements are crucial in defining how leaders and their teams interact, overcome challenges, and achieve goals.

Traits of Effective Leaders and Followers

- Integrity: Both leaders and followers must possess a strong sense of integrity. Leaders are expected to be honest and transparent in their actions, setting a moral compass for the organization. Similarly, followers with integrity contribute to a trustworthy and ethical work environment.

- Empathy: The ability to understand and share the feelings of others is vital. Empathetic leaders can build strong relationships, understand team members' needs, and foster a supportive culture. Followers also benefit from empathy, as it enhances teamwork and cooperation.

- Resilience: In the face of setbacks or failures, resilience allows leaders and followers alike to bounce back and learn from their experiences. This trait is essential for navigating the ups and downs of organizational life.

Skills of Effective Leaders and Followers

- Communication: Effective communication skills are paramount. Leaders must be able to convey their vision, give clear instructions, and listen to feedback. Followers need good communication skills to understand directives, provide meaningful feedback, and engage in constructive dialogue.

- Problem-Solving: Leaders are often required to make difficult decisions and solve complex problems. Likewise, followers who can think critically and offer solutions are invaluable to a team.

- Adaptability: The ability to adapt to changing circumstances and environments is crucial for both leaders and followers. This skill ensures that the team can pivot strategies or processes effectively when necessary.

Attitudes of Effective Leaders and Followers

- Openness to Learning: A leader who is open to learning and development sets a positive example for their team, promoting a culture of continuous improvement. Followers with a similar attitude contribute to an environment where growth is encouraged and valued.

- Collaborative Spirit: Successful leaders and followers understand the importance of collaboration. Leaders who promote teamwork foster an inclusive atmosphere, while followers who are willing to collaborate contribute to a more cohesive and effective team.

- Accountability: Leaders should hold themselves accountable for their decisions and actions, setting a precedent for their followers. Similarly, followers who take responsibility for their work and actions strengthen the team's overall performance.

The blend of these traits, skills, and attitudes in both leaders and followers creates a synergistic relationship that drives organizational success. Effective leadership is not just about the leader; it's also about fostering a team of effective followers who share a common vision and values.

Leadership, inherently adaptable, manifests differently across various environmental contexts, reflecting the unique challenges and dynamics of each setting. In team environments, leadership is often characterized by direct interaction and a hands-on approach. Effective team leaders excel in identifying individual strengths, fostering collaboration, and ensuring clear communication. The intimate scale of teams often allows for a more participative leadership style, where each member's input is crucial and valued.

When the scope expands to an organizational level, leadership adopts a more strategic character. Here, leaders are tasked with navigating the intricacies of organizational structures, cultures, and politics. They are responsible for setting visions, aligning the organization's goals with overarching values, and driving significant change initiatives. This larger scale demands that leaders balance internal management with external factors such as market trends and competition, necessitating a blend of visionary thinking and operational acumen.

At the societal level, leadership transcends organizational confines, involving the guidance and influence over broader populations. Leaders in this realm must possess a profound understanding of social dynamics, public policies, and economic trends. Their decisions and actions often shape public opinion, policy-making, and social movements, requiring a vision that extends far beyond the immediate horizon. This form of leadership carries a substantial ethical responsibility, as its impact is widespread and often enduring.

The key to effective leadership across these varying contexts lies in adaptability. The approach that works within a small team, centered around collaboration and shared responsibility, might need adjustment in a larger organizational setting where more directive strategies are necessary. Similarly, the broad-scale, visionary thinking essential for societal leadership contrasts with the more focused, operational mindset required at the team or organizational levels.

Leadership is a multifaceted endeavor, changing its shape and form to fit the context in which it operates. Whether guiding a team, an organization, or influencing societal change, effective leadership requires an understanding of the unique challenges and opportunities present in each environment. This adaptability ensures that leaders can effectively navigate and guide their respective domains towards success and meaningful impact.

The influence of technological advancements on leadership styles and strategies has been profound and far-reaching. In the modern era, technology is not just a tool for operational efficiency; it has become a critical factor in shaping how leaders communicate, make decisions, and strategize for the future.

One of the most significant impacts of technology on leadership is in the realm of communication. Digital platforms, social media, and collaborative tools have revolutionized the way leaders interact with their teams and stakeholders. These technologies facilitate faster, more efficient, and often more transparent communication. They enable leaders to connect with their teams regardless of geographical boundaries, fostering a more inclusive and diverse workplace.

Decision-making processes have also been transformed by technology. The availability of big data and advanced analytics tools allows leaders to make more informed, data-driven decisions. By leveraging these technologies, leaders can gain deeper insights into market trends, customer preferences, and internal performance metrics, leading to more strategic and effective decision-making.

Technology has enabled new leadership strategies, particularly in terms of remote and flexible working arrangements. The rise of remote work technologies has allowed leaders to manage dispersed teams effectively, breaking down traditional office barriers and introducing new dynamics in team management and collaboration. It has demanded that leaders be more adaptable and agile. The rapid pace of technological change means that leaders must be continuous learners, staying abreast of new tools and trends that can impact their organization. They must be able to lead their organizations through digital transformations, which often require significant cultural and operational shifts.

In the context of innovation, technology empowers leaders to foster a culture of innovation within their organizations. By embracing technological advancements, leaders can encourage experimentation, support new ideas, and drive innovation to maintain a competitive edge in their respective industries.

Globalization has had a significant impact on leadership practices and theories, fundamentally altering how leaders operate in today's interconnected world. The increasing integration of economies, cultures, and people brought about by globalization requires leaders to navigate a more complex and diverse global landscape.

One of the primary impacts of globalization on leadership is the need for cultural intelligence and sensitivity. Leaders must now be adept at understanding and respecting different cultural norms, practices, and perspectives. This skill is essential for effective communication, team-building, and conflict resolution in a multicultural environment. Leaders must be able to adapt their style and approach to be effective across various cultural contexts.

Another consequence of globalization is the expansion of organizational operations across borders. Leaders often find themselves managing geographically dispersed teams or multinational operations. This requires a nuanced understanding of global markets, as well as the ability to effectively manage remote teams, often with different working styles and time zones.

Globalization has also influenced leadership theories by emphasizing the importance of collaborative and participative leadership styles. In a globalized world, top-down, hierarchical leadership is less effective. Instead, leaders are expected to foster collaboration, encourage input from diverse team members, and facilitate inclusive decision-making processes. It has brought about increased competition and rapid market changes, necessitating agile and adaptive leadership. Leaders must be able to quickly respond to global market trends, economic shifts, and international events. This environment demands that leaders are not only strategic thinkers but also capable of implementing rapid changes and innovations.

Ethical leadership has become more pronounced in the context of globalization. Leaders must now consider the global impact of their decisions, including environmental, social, and governance aspects. Ethical considerations, corporate social responsibility, and sustainability are increasingly important in leadership practices and decisions.

Globalization has broadened the scope of leadership, introducing new challenges and opportunities. Today's leaders must be culturally intelligent, adept at managing diversity, agile in their decision-making, and committed to ethical standards that resonate on a global scale. These changes have led to a transformation in leadership practices and theories, emphasizing adaptability, collaboration, and ethical responsibility in a global context.

The COVID-19 pandemic has had a profound and immediate impact on organizational structures and leadership roles, prompting a swift and often drastic reevaluation of how businesses operate and how leaders guide their teams. The pandemic's onset brought about unprecedented challenges that necessitated quick adaptation and resilience from both organizations and their leaders.

One of the most significant immediate effects was the shift to remote work. As governments imposed lockdowns and social distancing measures, organizations had to rapidly transition to a remote working model. This change disrupted traditional office-based structures and required leaders to manage teams virtually. The shift posed logistical challenges in terms of technology infrastructure and necessitated a change in communication styles and methods.

Leadership roles also evolved in response to the pandemic. There was an increased emphasis on empathetic and supportive leadership, as leaders had to address not only the professional but also the personal and emotional well-being of their employees. The crisis highlighted the need for leaders to be more than just decision-makers; they had to be empathizers, communicators, and motivators in the face of uncertainty and stress.

The pandemic also accelerated the adoption of digital technologies. Organizations had to quickly embrace digital tools for collaboration, communication, and operation to maintain continuity. This digital transformation pushed leaders to swiftly upskill and become adept at using these technologies, not just for operational efficiency but also for maintaining team cohesion and morale.

Another immediate effect was on decision-making processes. The fast-evolving nature of the pandemic required leaders to make quick and often difficult decisions regarding business operations, employee safety, and financial management. This situation demanded a more agile and responsive leadership approach, with an emphasis on rapid decision-making and flexibility.

Organizational structures became more fluid and less hierarchical. The crisis necessitated a breakdown of silos and a move towards more collaborative and cross-functional teams. Leaders had to foster a culture of innovation and adaptability, encouraging teams to find new solutions to unprecedented problems.

The pandemic brought to the fore the importance of crisis management and contingency planning in leadership roles. Leaders had to develop and implement effective crisis management strategies, ensuring clear communication and a swift response to the changing situation. This aspect of leadership involved not just navigating the organization through the crisis but also preparing for post-pandemic recovery and future resilience.

The COVID-19 pandemic has catalyzed long-term changes and adaptations in the business world, some of which are likely to persist far beyond the immediate crisis. These transformations have reshaped the landscape of work, leadership, and organizational dynamics.

Perhaps the most enduring change is the widespread shift to remote work. What began as a temporary solution has evolved into a new norm for many organizations. This shift has significant implications for workplace culture, communication methods, and work-life balance. Companies are rethinking their need for physical office spaces, leading to a reevaluation of real estate investments and office designs. Moreover, this shift has demonstrated the potential for a more flexible workforce, challenging the traditional 9-to-5 workday and offering employees greater autonomy over their schedules.

The pandemic accelerated digital transformation across various sectors. Businesses have rapidly adopted digital tools and platforms for collaboration, project management, customer engagement, and e-commerce. This digital leap forward has also prompted changes in IT infrastructure and cybersecurity measures, as organizations seek to support remote work and protect against increased cyber threats. Leaders and employees alike have had to upskill to adapt to these digital tools, leading to a greater focus on digital literacy and continuous learning within organizations.

Employee expectations regarding work have also evolved. There's an increasing demand for flexibility, work-life balance, and a greater focus on employee well-being. Employees are seeking more meaningful and engaging work experiences, where their contributions are recognized, and their wellness is prioritized. This shift has prompted leaders to place more emphasis on mental health, create more inclusive and supportive workplace cultures, and reconsider employee benefits and policies.

Leadership roles have adapted in response to these changes. Leaders are now expected to be more empathetic, adaptable, and digitally savvy. They must lead with a human touch, balancing productivity with empathy and understanding. The pandemic has highlighted the importance of transparent and frequent communication, resilience in the face of uncertainty, and the ability to inspire and motivate teams remotely.
Organizational Structure and Strategy

Organizational structures have become more agile and less hierarchical. There's a greater focus on cross-functional teams, decentralization, and empowerment at various levels. Companies are also revisiting their business models and strategies to adapt to the changed economic landscape, with many diversifying their offerings or accelerating their digital services.

The pandemic has fundamentally altered perceptions of the future of work. There's a growing recognition of the potential for remote and hybrid work models, a greater reliance on digital technologies, and an emphasis on agility and resilience in business strategies. The lasting changes and adaptations brought about by the COVID-19 pandemic have set the stage for a new era of work. This era is characterized by flexibility, digital integration, evolving employee expectations, and a reimagined approach to leadership and organizational structure. These changes are not just reactive measures but are shaping the future trajectory of how organizations operate and compete.

In the wake of ongoing changes, particularly those accelerated by the COVID-19 pandemic, the need for adaptable, flexible, and relational leadership styles has become more pronounced than ever. The rapidly evolving business landscape, characterized by uncertainty and constant change, requires leaders who can not only navigate but also thrive in such environments.

Adaptability in leadership refers to the ability to adjust strategies, goals, and tactics in response to changing circumstances. This trait has become indispensable in today's dynamic business world. Adaptable leaders are those who can pivot quickly in response to new challenges, opportunities, and information. They are open to new ideas, willing to abandon outdated practices, and are constantly seeking innovative solutions. Adaptable leaders are also skilled at leading their organizations through transitions, be it a shift to remote work, a change in business model, or navigating market fluctuations.

Flexibility in leadership goes hand in hand with adaptability but focuses more on the willingness and ability to change one's leadership style and approach based on the situation and the needs of the team. Flexible leaders are not wedded to a single leadership style; they can move fluidly between authoritative, collaborative, and supportive styles as the context demands. This flexibility is crucial in managing diverse teams, as it allows leaders to meet varying individual and collective needs, fostering a more inclusive and effective work environment.

Relational leadership emphasizes the importance of building strong, positive relationships with and among team members. It involves creating a supportive environment where open communication, mutual respect, and trust are paramount. In times of change and uncertainty, relational leadership becomes even more vital as it helps in maintaining team cohesion and morale. Leaders who prioritize relationships can better understand their team members' concerns, motivations, and needs, enabling them to lead in a more empathetic and effective manner.

Navigating Ongoing Changes

The ongoing changes in the business world, including technological advancements, evolving market conditions, and shifts in workplace dynamics, necessitate leaders who can employ these adaptable, flexible, and relational styles. Such leaders are better equipped to guide their organizations through the complexities of the modern business environment. They can foster a culture of agility and resilience, ensuring that their organizations are not just reactive to changes but are also proactive in capitalizing on new opportunities.

Adaptable, flexible, and relational leadership styles are essential in today's ever-changing business landscape. Leaders who embody these qualities are more capable of navigating their organizations through uncertainty, fostering innovation, and maintaining strong, effective teams. As the business world continues to evolve, these leadership styles will become increasingly important for sustainable success and growth.

In the rapidly evolving and often unpredictable business world of today, the ability of an organization to develop resilience and agility has become a crucial focus for effective leadership. Organizational resilience is the capability to withstand, adapt, and recover from adversities and challenges, while agility is about responding swiftly and effectively to change. These two qualities are essential for navigating the complexities and uncertainties of the modern business landscape.

Organizational resilience is not merely about enduring difficulties but also about emerging stronger from them. This requires a culture that views challenges as opportunities for learning and growth. Leaders play a vital role in fostering this resilience by encouraging a mindset of continuous improvement and adaptability. This involves promoting innovation, supporting risk-taking, and embedding the learning from failures into the organization's fabric. Resilient organizations are also characterized by robust networks and relationships, both internally and externally, providing crucial support during times of crisis.

Alongside resilience, agility within an organization is paramount. It encompasses more than just speed; it's about being nimble and responsive to market changes, technological advancements, and evolving customer preferences. Agile organizations can pivot quickly in response to new opportunities or threats. Leaders can cultivate this agility by streamlining decision-making processes, encouraging collaboration across different functions, and fostering an environment where feedback is actively sought and promptly acted upon. Technological adoption is also a key element in enhancing organizational agility, facilitating the ability to adapt operations swiftly.

While resilience focuses on stability and endurance and agility on change and movement, these attributes are complementary. A resilient organization provides a stable foundation necessary for agility, allowing for rapid movement and adaptation when needed. Conversely, agility can bolster resilience, ensuring that an organization can adjust quickly and effectively to withstand challenges.

Effective leadership in this context is about creating a culture that balances both stability and dynamism. It involves building an organization capable of withstanding shocks and learning from these experiences while remaining agile enough to seize new opportunities. This balanced approach is increasingly crucial for sustaining success in an ever-changing and complex business environment.

The growing importance of inclusivity and diversity in effective leadership has become increasingly recognized in the contemporary business landscape. In a world characterized by global interconnectedness and a diverse workforce, leaders who embrace and leverage diversity and inclusivity are better positioned to drive innovation, creativity, and organizational success.

Inclusivity in leadership refers to the practice of making all members of an organization feel valued and included, irrespective of their background, identity, or perspective. This approach goes beyond mere tolerance or acceptance; it involves actively seeking out, appreciating, and utilizing the diverse skills, experiences, and viewpoints that each individual brings to the table. Inclusive leaders create environments where differences are celebrated, and every individual feels empowered to contribute to their fullest potential.

Diversity in leadership is equally crucial. It encompasses a broad range of dimensions, including but not limited to race, gender, age, ethnicity, sexual orientation, and cultural background. Diverse leadership teams are more representative of the broader society and the global marketplace. They bring a variety of perspectives and problem-solving approaches, which can lead to more innovative and effective decision-making. Research has consistently shown that organizations with diverse leadership are more successful, more adaptable to change, and better at identifying and capitalizing on new opportunities.

The benefits of inclusivity and diversity in leadership extend beyond organizational walls. They foster a positive and progressive company image, attracting talent from a wider pool and appealing to a broader customer base. In today's socially conscious market, customers and clients often prefer to engage with companies that demonstrate a commitment to diversity and inclusivity.

Inclusive and diverse leadership is critical in navigating the complexities of a globalized business environment. Leaders who understand and appreciate cultural nuances and global perspectives can better manage international teams, enter new markets, and create products and services that resonate across cultures. The push for inclusivity and diversity also reflects a broader societal shift towards equality and social justice. Leaders have a responsibility to drive this change within their organizations, creating workplaces that are not only diverse and inclusive but also equitable and just.

Our book "Leadership Transformed: Strategies for the Next Generation of Organizational Excellence" is structured to provide a comprehensive exploration of modern leadership dynamics. Here's an overview of the subsequent chapters, each focusing on a key theme or area crucial to understanding and practicing effective leadership in today's rapidly changing world.

1. Leadership and Motivation in a Post-COVID World: This chapter examines how the pandemic has reshaped the landscape of work and leadership, focusing on new approaches to motivation and the evolving role of leaders in these challenging times.

2. Team Dynamics, Innovation, and Remote Work: Delving into the complexities of managing teams in a remote or hybrid environment, this chapter explores strategies for maintaining innovation and collaboration when traditional office settings are no longer the norm.

3. Organizational Culture and Agile Change Management: Here, the focus shifts to the importance of building an adaptable organizational culture, capable of responding swiftly to changes, and the role of leaders in guiding their organizations through these transitions.

4. Complex Human Behaviors and New Work Realities: This chapter provides insights into the intricate human behaviors within organizations, particularly in the context of new work realities shaped by technological advancements and evolving societal norms.

5. Leadership in Diverse and Flexible Work Modes: Addressing the challenges and opportunities presented by diverse work modes, this chapter discusses the need for leadership styles that are flexible and adaptable to various working conditions and team compositions.

6. Diversity, Equity, and Inclusion in Leadership: Emphasizing the growing importance of inclusivity and diversity, this chapter explores how leaders can foster environments that value and leverage diverse perspectives and backgrounds.

7. Technology-Driven Leadership: Focusing on the impact of technological advancements, this chapter discusses how leaders can harness technology for better decision-making, enhanced efficiency, and fostering a culture of innovation.

8. Global Leadership in Multicultural Settings: This chapter covers the nuances of leading in a globalized world, offering strategies for managing multicultural teams and navigating the complexities of international business.

9. Emerging Leadership Approaches: Looking towards the future, this chapter introduces new and emerging leadership theories and practices, highlighting how they can be applied to meet the challenges of a rapidly changing business landscape.

10. Conclusion: The Future of Leadership: The concluding chapter summarizes the key insights from the book and looks ahead at the potential future developments in leadership and organizational dynamics.

Each chapter of "Leadership Transformed" is designed to provide in-depth knowledge, practical strategies, and thought-provoking insights, equipping current and aspiring leaders with the tools needed to navigate the complexities of modern organizational leadership.

In our book readers are invited on an enlightening journey through the multifaceted world of modern leadership. This journey offers a wealth of practical knowledge, strategies, and insights designed to equip current and aspiring leaders with the tools necessary to navigate and excel in today's complex organizational landscapes.

As readers delve into the book, they will gain a deeper understanding of how the COVID-19 pandemic has reshaped the workplace and leadership roles. They will learn about new approaches to motivate and engage teams in a world that has rapidly shifted to remote and hybrid working models. This exploration provides valuable insights into maintaining team cohesion and productivity despite physical distances.

We offer strategies for building adaptable and agile organizational cultures. Readers will discover how to effectively manage change in fast-paced environments, fostering resilience and flexibility within their teams and organizations. This knowledge is crucial for leaders looking to guide their teams through uncertainties and challenges. In addition to these macro-level strategies, the book provides a granular look at human behavior within organizational settings. Readers will learn about the dynamics of human interactions at work, gaining insights into effective communication, conflict resolution, and fostering a collaborative work environment.

A significant portion of the book is dedicated to understanding and implementing inclusive and diverse leadership practices. Readers will learn the importance of creating an environment where every team member feels valued and how diverse perspectives can lead to more innovative solutions and a stronger organizational performance. Technological advancements and their impact on leadership form another key area of learning. The book guides readers through the ways technology can enhance decision-making processes, improve efficiency, and drive innovation. This knowledge is vital for leaders looking to leverage technology for their organization's advantage.

For those navigating the global business arena, the book offers strategies for leading diverse and geographically dispersed teams, providing insights into the complexities and rewards of global leadership. Looking to the future, readers will explore emerging leadership theories and practices, preparing them for the evolving challenges of the business world. This future-focused perspective ensures that leaders can stay ahead of the curve and continue to grow in their roles.

We synthesize these insights, offering readers a comprehensive understanding of modern leadership. "Leadership Transformed" is more than just a guide; it's a resource packed with actionable advice, real-world examples, and thought-provoking ideas that will inspire and empower leaders at all levels. Readers can expect to close the book with a richer understanding of what it means to be a leader today and how they can apply these lessons to lead with greater impact, resilience, and vision in their own professional journeys.

In this introductory chapter we have laid the foundational framework for understanding the complex and dynamic nature of modern leadership. The chapter began by setting the scene, highlighting the evolving world of leadership and emphasizing the need for new strategies and approaches in the face of global changes and challenges. The historical and global perspective on leadership was then explored, tracing the evolution of leadership theories and practices from their early incarnations to their current state. This overview provided a backdrop for understanding how leadership has adapted and transformed across different cultures and eras. Following this, we introduced the concept of leadership as a dynamic and relational process. It delved into the multifaceted nature of leadership, discussing how effective leadership involves not just directing or managing but fostering relationships, understanding team dynamics, and adapting to various situations.

The chapter also examined the essential traits, skills, and attitudes that constitute effective leadership and followership. The discussion highlighted attributes such as integrity, empathy, resilience, communication, problem-solving, adaptability, openness to learning, a collaborative spirit, and accountability, demonstrating how these qualities are critical in both leaders and followers for organizational success.

Next, our introduction addressed how leadership varies in different environmental contexts – teams, organizations, and societal levels. It provided insights into the unique challenges and approaches required in each of these settings, emphasizing the need for leaders to adapt their styles and strategies according to the situation.

We then discussed the influence of technological advancements on leadership styles and strategies, underscoring how technology has become a pivotal element in modern leadership, affecting communication, decision-making, and organizational dynamics. The introductory chapter set the stage for a deeper exploration into modern leadership. It established the key themes of adaptability, relational dynamics, environmental context, and the impact of technology, all of which are crucial for understanding and excelling in today's leadership roles. This chapter serves as a gateway into the nuanced and ever-evolving world of leadership, setting the tone for the comprehensive journey that "Leadership Transformed" promises to take its readers on.

Having established a foundational understanding of the dynamic and multifaceted nature of modern leadership in this introductory chapter, we now stand at the threshold of a deeper exploration into one of the most pivotal and timely aspects of contemporary leadership: Leadership and Motivation in a Post-COVID World.

The next chapter promises to delve into the intricacies of how the COVID-19 pandemic has not only disrupted the traditional paradigms of work and leadership but also brought about a paradigm shift in how leaders inspire and motivate their teams in these unprecedented times. We will explore the challenges and opportunities that have emerged in the wake of the pandemic, examining how the crisis has reshaped the workplace, redefined employee expectations, and necessitated a reevaluation of motivational strategies.

As we transition into this exploration, readers can anticipate a rich tapestry of insights and strategies tailored to navigating the post-pandemic landscape. The upcoming chapter will offer practical guidance on adapting leadership styles to meet the evolving needs of teams, fostering resilience, and maintaining motivation amidst ongoing uncertainties and changes. Prepare to embark on a journey that will not only deepen your understanding of the complexities of leading in a post-COVID world but also equip you with the tools to effectively motivate and guide your teams through the challenges and opportunities of this new era. The insights gleaned in the next chapter are essential for any leader seeking to navigate the post-pandemic landscape with confidence, empathy, and effectiveness.

1. Leadership and Motivation in a Post-COVID World

As the world gradually emerges from the shadows of the COVID-19 pandemic, it is ushering in an era that presents novel challenges and opportunities for leadership and motivation. This chapter aims to unravel the complex tapestry of post-COVID leadership, exploring how the pandemic has not only reshaped the corporate landscape but also redefined the essence of effective leadership and employee motivation.

The onset of the pandemic was a moment of unprecedented change. Organizations worldwide found themselves navigating uncharted waters, grappling with rapid shifts to remote work, fluctuating market demands, and the overarching need to ensure employee safety and well-being. This period of crisis and adaptation has left an indelible mark on the world of work, fundamentally altering how leaders engage with and motivate their teams.

In this new landscape, the conventional models of leadership have been put to the test. The crisis underscored the need for leaders who are not just strategic thinkers and decision-makers but also empathizers, communicators, and caretakers. The qualities of resilience, adaptability, and emotional intelligence have risen to the forefront, proving essential for navigating through times of uncertainty and change.

The pandemic has shifted the dynamics of employee motivation. Traditional motivators such as job security and financial incentives, while still relevant, are now part of a broader spectrum that includes work-life balance, mental health, and a sense of purpose and belonging. Leaders are now tasked with understanding and addressing these diverse motivational drivers in a landscape where the boundaries between personal and professional life have blurred.

This chapter will delve into these transformed paradigms, examining the new skills and approaches that leaders must adopt to effectively guide their teams in the post-COVID era. It will explore strategies for maintaining team cohesion and motivation in a hybrid or fully remote work environment and discuss how leaders can foster a culture of resilience and continuous adaptation. The insights provided here are not just a reflection on a crisis but a roadmap for the future, offering guidance on how to lead and motivate in a world that continues to evolve in the wake of COVID-19.

One of the most significant changes has been the widespread transition to remote work. Organizations around the globe were compelled to adapt swiftly to this new mode, transitioning from traditional office environments to virtual platforms. This shift didn't merely change the physical location of work but also revolutionized work methodologies, altering team interactions, communication modes, and collaborative practices. Accompanying this change was a profound evolution in workplace cultures and practices. Organizations had to innovate their approach to managing workflows, engaging employees, and evaluating performance, all within a remote context. The blurring lines between personal and professional life brought forth a new emphasis on work-life balance, demanding adjustments in organizational culture and management practices.

The pandemic also cast a spotlight on the mental and emotional well-being of employees. Leaders found themselves navigating not only the physical health concerns related to the pandemic but also addressing the psychological impacts such as isolation and stress. This situation called for a leadership approach that was more compassionate and empathetic, recognizing the holistic well-being of team members.

Another significant development was the accelerated pace of digital transformation. The necessity to operate remotely led to an increased reliance on digital tools for basic operational needs, pushing both leaders and employees to rapidly adapt to these technologies.

Employee expectations from their workplaces underwent a dramatic transformation. The pandemic era saw a shift in priorities, with employees seeking greater flexibility, meaningful engagement, organizational values alignment, and supportive work environments. This change in expectations necessitated a reevaluation of what motivates and satisfies employees in their professional roles.

The economic and market uncertainties triggered by the pandemic have led to fluctuations in consumer behaviors, disruptions in supply chains, and shifts in business models. Leaders have been required to navigate these uncertainties with agility and foresight, ensuring business continuity and organizational resilience in a highly volatile environment. As we venture into the heart of this chapter, our focus narrows to examine how crucial aspects of leadership and motivation have shifted in the 'new normal' established by the COVID-19 pandemic. This exploration is essential, as the profound changes brought about by the pandemic have redefined what effective leadership looks like in contemporary organizational settings.

In this new landscape, leaders are called upon to navigate a series of unprecedented challenges and transformations. The abrupt shift to remote work, the urgent need for digital proficiency, the reevaluation of workplace cultures, and the heightened emphasis on employee well-being – all these elements have combined to create a new paradigm for leadership.

This chapter delves into these transformed dynamics, seeking to understand how leaders can effectively guide their teams in a world where the only constant is change. It examines the adaptations necessary in leadership styles to meet the evolving needs and expectations of teams and organizations. The focus is not only on overcoming the immediate challenges posed by the pandemic but also on leveraging these changes as opportunities for growth and innovation. As we navigate through this chapter, we will explore how leaders can foster resilience and agility in their teams, ensuring that organizations are not just surviving but thriving in this new environment. We will also look at how the pandemic has accelerated the transition to more empathetic and inclusive leadership, where understanding and addressing the diverse needs of employees is paramount.

This chapter will also shed light on the crucial role of motivation in this new context. With traditional motivators being redefined, leaders must find novel ways to inspire and engage their teams, ensuring productivity and satisfaction in a landscape marked by uncertainty and continuous adaptation.

Before delving into the shifts in motivational theories and practices in the post-COVID era, it's crucial to understand the traditional frameworks that have shaped our understanding of motivation in the workplace. These pre-COVID motivational theories and practices laid the groundwork for how leaders and organizations approached employee motivation and job satisfaction.

Maslow's Hierarchy of Needs

One of the foundational theories of motivation is Abraham Maslow's Hierarchy of Needs, introduced in the 1940s. Maslow proposed that human beings have a hierarchy of needs, starting from basic physiological needs to safety, love/belonging, esteem, and self-actualization. In the workplace, this theory suggested that employees must have their basic needs met before they can be motivated by higher-level needs like recognition and personal development.

Herzberg's Two-Factor Theory

Developed in the 1950s by Frederick Herzberg, this theory, also known as the Motivation-Hygiene Theory, posits that there are two factors that influence employee motivation and satisfaction: hygiene factors and motivators. Hygiene factors, such as salary and work conditions, do not necessarily motivate employees but can cause dissatisfaction if inadequate. Motivators, such as recognition and challenging work, drive job satisfaction and motivation.

McGregor's Theory X and Theory Y

In the 1960s, Douglas McGregor introduced these two contrasting theories of human work motivation. Theory X assumes that employees are inherently lazy and will avoid work if they can. In contrast, Theory Y suggests that employees are naturally motivated to work and seek out responsibility. These theories influenced managerial styles – either authoritarian (Theory X) or participative (Theory Y).

Vroom's Expectancy Theory

Victor Vroom's theory, formulated in the 1960s, is based on the belief that employee effort will lead to performance and performance will lead to rewards. This theory posits that motivation is a result of how much an individual wants a reward (Valence), the assessment that the effort will lead to expected performance (Expectancy), and the belief that performance will lead to a reward (Instrumentality).

These theories collectively provided a diverse perspective on what motivates people at work. They emphasized various factors, from basic needs and job satisfaction to the influence of management styles and the relationship between effort, performance, and rewards. Understanding these traditional motivational theories is essential in appreciating how the context of motivation has evolved in the post-COVID world. The pandemic has not only changed the workplace environment but also influenced how these classic theories might be interpreted or applied in the contemporary context, a transition that we will explore in the following sections.

There are several modern evolving concepts and frameworks that can be viewed as emerging theories or adaptations of existing theories in response to the changed workplace dynamics or post-COVID-19. Here are a few such concepts:

Digital Engagement Theory

This concept focuses on motivating employees through digital mediums. It explores how digital tools can be used for engagement, recognition, and creating a sense of community among remote workers. This theory adapts elements of traditional engagement theories to the digital and remote work environment.

The Theory of Agile Leadership

Stemming from Agile Management principles, this theory suggests that motivation in the workplace is enhanced by agile leadership practices, such as flexibility, adaptability, and a focus on continuous improvement. It posits that an agile environment, characterized by rapid response to change and employee empowerment, can significantly boost motivation and job satisfaction.

Eudaimonic Well-being in the Workplace

Building on the concept of eudaimonia (a term from Aristotelian philosophy referring to happiness derived from fulfilling one's potential), this theory suggests that post-COVID motivation is driven by opportunities for personal and professional growth, meaningful work, and contributing to a larger purpose.

Psychological Safety and Resilience Theory

This theory combines the importance of psychological safety (a concept popularized by Amy Edmondson) with resilience. It suggests that post-pandemic motivation is enhanced in environments where employees feel safe to take risks and express themselves without fear of negative consequences, and where they are supported to build resilience in the face of challenges.

Hybrid Workforce Motivation Theory

This emerging theory explores the motivational dynamics in a hybrid workforce (a mix of remote and in-office employees). It suggests that motivation in such settings is driven by factors like flexibility, autonomy, and the balance between digital connectivity and face-to-face interactions.

Sustainable Motivation Theory

Emerging from the growing emphasis on sustainability and corporate social responsibility, this theory posits that employees are increasingly motivated by working in organizations that prioritize sustainable practices and contribute positively to social and environmental issues.

These evolving concepts reflect an adaptation of traditional motivational theories to the unique circumstances and challenges of the post-COVID era, emphasizing flexibility, digital engagement, psychological well-being, and a sense of purpose and sustainability. They offer a contemporary framework for understanding what drives and inspires employees in today's rapidly changing work environment.

The pandemic has not only changed the way we work but also shifted the needs, values, and motivations of employees in profound ways. One of the most noticeable changes has been in the realm of work-life balance. The blending of personal and professional lives, especially for those working remotely, has led to a reevaluation of what work-life balance means. Employees are increasingly seeking flexibility in their work schedules and arrangements, valuing the autonomy to manage their time and responsibilities. It has also heightened the focus on health and well-being. Employees are more conscious of their physical and mental health, leading to a demand for better health benefits, mental health support, and wellness programs in the workplace. There's a greater expectation for employers to not only acknowledge these concerns but actively support their employees' well-being.

Another shift has been towards a greater need for job security and stability. The economic uncertainties brought about by the pandemic have made job security a more prominent motivator. Employees are looking for assurances of stability and transparency from their employers about the future of their roles and the organization.

The value placed on meaningful work has also intensified. The pandemic, for many, has been a period of reflection on personal and professional goals. Employees are increasingly motivated by work that they find fulfilling and that aligns with their personal values and goals. There's a stronger desire to contribute to something larger than oneself, be it social causes, community well-being, or impactful organizational projects.

In terms of professional development, the rapid changes in the business landscape have underscored the importance of continuous learning and adaptability. Employees are motivated by opportunities for growth, upskilling, and developing new competencies that align with the evolving demands of the post-pandemic world. Communication and connection have also emerged as key motivators. With many teams working remotely, there's a heightened need for effective communication and a sense of connection with colleagues and the organization. Employees are looking for leaders who can effectively communicate, build team cohesion, and foster a sense of belonging, even in a remote setting.

The pandemic has introduced new challenges in motivating employees, significantly altering the traditional dynamics of the workplace. Among these challenges, remote work fatigue, the blurring lines of work-life balance, and heightened mental health concerns stand out as key areas that leaders and organizations must address to maintain employee motivation and well-being.

Remote Work Fatigue

One of the most prevalent challenges in the post-COVID work environment is remote work fatigue. The novelty of working from home has, for many, given way to a sense of weariness. Constant virtual meetings, the lack of physical separation between work and personal life, and the absence of informal, social interactions that the office environment provided have contributed to a sense of burnout among employees. This fatigue can lead to decreased motivation, lower productivity, and a disconnection from the team and organizational goals.

Work-Life Balance

The pandemic has significantly blurred the lines between work and personal life, especially for those working from home. The flexibility of remote work can often translate into longer working hours and the expectation of being constantly available. This erosion of boundaries can lead to stress and burnout, making it challenging for employees to stay motivated. Finding the right balance where flexibility does not impinge on personal time is critical for maintaining motivation and productivity.

Mental Health Concerns

The pandemic has also brought mental health concerns to the forefront. The isolation of remote work, anxiety about the pandemic itself, concerns about job security, and the challenges of juggling work with home responsibilities (like childcare) have taken a toll on employees' mental health. These issues can significantly impact an employee's motivation and engagement with their work.

Addressing these challenges requires a multifaceted approach. For remote work fatigue, organizations can introduce measures to reduce the strain, such as flexible scheduling, encouraging regular breaks, setting boundaries for work hours, and reducing the dependency on virtual meetings by promoting asynchronous communication.

To improve work-life balance, leaders can set clear expectations regarding work hours, respect personal time, and model this behavior themselves. Encouraging employees to establish a dedicated workspace, if possible, and recognizing the need for flexible work arrangements can also help.

Addressing mental health concerns involves creating a supportive work environment where mental health is openly discussed and destigmatized. Providing access to mental health resources, offering wellness programs, and ensuring employees have someone to talk to about their concerns are critical steps. Leaders should be trained to recognize signs of mental health struggles and be equipped to guide employees to the help they need.

In this new context shaped by the pandemic, leaders face the challenge of keeping their teams motivated amidst remote work fatigue, disrupted work-life balance, and prevalent mental health concerns. To navigate this effectively, leaders can employ a range of practical strategies centered around empathy, flexibility, and robust support systems.

1. Empathy in Leadership: Leaders should cultivate an empathetic approach, which involves actively listening to their team members' concerns and understanding their unique situations. Regular check-ins that go beyond work-related discussions can help leaders gauge the well-being of their team members. Showing genuine concern and understanding for the challenges that employees face, both professionally and personally, can foster a supportive and motivating work environment.

2. Promoting Flexibility: Flexibility is key in the post-pandemic workplace. Leaders should recognize that a one-size-fits-all approach may not work in these times. Allowing flexible work hours, acknowledging the need for occasional breaks, and being understanding when life interferes with work can go a long way in maintaining motivation. This flexibility can manifest in various forms, from adapting deadlines to accommodating different working styles.

3. Building Robust Support Systems: Creating strong support systems within the organization is crucial. This can include

setting up peer support groups, offering mentorship programs, or providing access to professional counseling services. Leaders should also ensure that employees are aware of and can easily access these resources.

4. Encouraging a Healthy Work-Life Balance: Leaders should lead by example in maintaining a healthy work-life balance, demonstrating to their team that it's okay to disconnect after work hours and during weekends. Encouraging employees to take their vacation time and disconnect from work can help prevent burnout.

5. Clear Communication and Setting Expectations: Transparent communication regarding organizational changes, job security, and future plans can alleviate anxiety and uncertainty. Leaders should clearly communicate expectations, changes in roles, or shifts in strategies to keep everyone aligned and motivated.

6. Recognition and Appreciation: Regularly recognizing and appreciating the hard work and achievements of team members can boost morale. This recognition can be through formal mechanisms like awards and bonuses or informal methods like shout-outs in team meetings or personal thank-you notes.

7. Professional Development Opportunities: Offering opportunities for professional growth and development can also be a strong motivator. Encouraging employees to take up online courses, attend webinars, or participate in virtual conferences can help them feel invested in and valued by the organization.

8. Fostering Team Connection and Cohesion: Finally, creating opportunities for virtual team-building activities can help maintain a sense of team cohesion and belonging. These activities can range from informal virtual coffee breaks to more structured team-building exercises.

By employing these strategies centered around empathy, flexibility, and strong support systems, leaders can effectively motivate and support their teams in this new and evolving work context.

Having explored the practical strategies for motivating teams in the post-pandemic context, it's important to shift our focus and provide a backdrop against which these contemporary approaches can be better understood. This backdrop is the realm of traditional leadership styles. By reviewing these styles, we gain context and a deeper appreciation for how leadership has evolved and adapted to the current landscape.

Traditional leadership styles have laid the groundwork for our understanding of leadership dynamics and have shaped organizational cultures for decades. These styles, each with its own unique characteristics and methodologies, have been instrumental in guiding leaders in their decision-making, team management, and strategic planning.

- Authoritarian Leadership: This style is characterized by strong control over all decisions and little input from team members. The leader dictates policies and procedures, decides what goals are to be achieved, and directs all the activities without any meaningful participation from subordinates.

- Democratic Leadership: Contrasting with authoritarian leadership, the democratic style involves sharing decision-making responsibilities with team members. This leader encourages participation and contribution from the group, fostering a more collaborative and inclusive environment. Decisions are made by consensus, and the input of team members is valued and considered.

- Laissez-Faire Leadership: The laissez-faire leader takes a hands-off approach, providing minimal direction and allowing team members to make decisions and solve problems on their own. This style is based on the belief that employees are capable of self-direction and prefer autonomy in their tasks.

- Transactional Leadership: This style is based on the concept of exchanges between the leader and the followers. Leaders provide clear instructions and expectations, and rewards or punishments are contingent on performance. This approach is often seen in organizations where results and efficiency are the primary focus.

- Transformational Leadership: Transformational leaders inspire and motivate their followers to achieve extraordinary outcomes and, in the process, develop their own leadership capacity. They focus on the bigger picture, initiate change, and inspire followers to commit to a shared vision and goals.

Reviewing these traditional leadership styles provides valuable context for understanding the evolution of leadership practices. It's clear that the rigid structures and defined roles of these traditional styles are being reshaped in the post-pandemic world. The shift towards more empathetic, flexible, and supportive leadership practices reflects a departure from some of these traditional methods. As we continue our exploration, we'll see how these classic styles are being adapted and reimagined to meet the needs of a rapidly changing and increasingly complex work environment.

In adapting to the demands of remote and hybrid work environments, leaders have undergone a significant transformation in their approach to management. This shift has been characterized by specific adaptations to ensure effective team management despite the physical distance. Communication has become more nuanced in the remote context. Leaders have moved beyond traditional emails and meetings, embracing a variety of digital tools like video conferencing, instant messaging, and collaborative platforms. They've learned to be more deliberate in their communication, ensuring clarity to avoid the pitfalls of miscommunication that can occur without the nuances of face-to-face interaction.

Trust and empowerment have emerged as cornerstones of remote leadership. With the absence of physical oversight, leaders have shifted their focus to outcomes rather than traditional metrics like hours logged. This approach involves granting team members more autonomy, trusting them to manage their schedules and workload effectively. It's a shift from micromanagement to a more results-oriented style.

Emotional intelligence has taken on a new level of importance. Leaders have had to develop a keener sense of empathy and understanding, recognizing that remote work can bring unique challenges such as isolation or burnout. They've become more attentive to these issues, regularly checking in with their team members not just about work but also their overall well-being. Adaptability and flexibility have become vital traits for leaders in remote settings. This flexibility manifests in various ways, from accommodating different time zones and work-life scenarios to being open to new methods and tools that enhance remote work efficiency. Creating a sense of community and team cohesion virtually has required creative thinking. Leaders have initiated virtual team-building activities and informal online social events. Celebrations of personal and professional milestones, once a part of office culture, have now found a new avatar in the digital workspace.

Professional development remains a priority, with leaders finding innovative ways to provide growth opportunities. This includes virtual training sessions, e-learning courses, and regular one-on-one career development discussions. Leaders have ensured that despite the distance, career progression and learning opportunities continue to be a focal point of their team's development.

Leveraging technology has gone beyond basic communication needs. Leaders have explored and integrated advanced project management tools, workflow tracking systems, and collaborative software to enhance productivity and streamline virtual operations.

The shift to virtual settings, expedited by the COVID-19 pandemic, has required leaders to rethink and reimagine their approaches to communication, team cohesion, and performance management.

Communication Challenges and Opportunities

In a virtual environment, the absence of face-to-face interactions and non-verbal cues can lead to misunderstandings and a sense of disconnect. Leaders must navigate these challenges by adopting clear, concise, and frequent communication. The opportunity here lies in leveraging various digital communication tools – from video calls to messaging platforms – to maintain regular contact and ensure clarity. Virtual communication also offers the flexibility to connect across geographies and time zones, potentially leading to more inclusive and diverse interactions.

Maintaining Team Cohesion

Building and sustaining team cohesion without the organic interactions that occur in physical office spaces is another challenge. Leaders in virtual settings must create a sense of belonging and community among team members who may feel isolated. This challenge is met by fostering an inclusive culture through virtual team-building activities, regular team meetings, and informal virtual gatherings. There is also an opportunity to harness diverse perspectives, as virtual teams can be more geographically and culturally diverse.

Performance Management in a Virtual Setting

Assessing and managing performance remotely requires a shift from traditional, oversight-based methods to a more results-oriented approach. The challenge for leaders is to ensure accountability and high performance without the ability to physically observe work processes. The key opportunity here is to focus on setting clear goals, providing regular feedback, and using technology to track progress. Virtual environments also allow for more flexible performance management practices, tailored to individual needs and working styles.

Adapting Leadership Style

Virtual environments necessitate an adaptive leadership style. Leaders must be empathetic to the unique circumstances and challenges faced by their team members. They should also be open to learning and adopting new technologies and methods to enhance team collaboration and productivity.

Leveraging Technology for Engagement

A significant opportunity in virtual settings is the use of technology not just for tasks and projects, but also for engaging and motivating team members. Innovative use of digital tools can create interactive and engaging experiences that foster team spirit and a sense of belonging.

Encouraging Self-Management and Autonomy

Virtual settings provide an opportunity for leaders to encourage greater self-management and autonomy among team members. By trusting employees to manage their work and time effectively, leaders can foster a culture of empowerment and responsibility.

The pandemic's impact on the workplace has led to notable examples and case studies of leaders who have successfully adapted their leadership styles in response to the challenges posed by remote work and the broader implications of COVID-19.

Satya Nadella - Microsoft: As the CEO of Microsoft, Satya Nadella demonstrated remarkable leadership in adapting to the pandemic. Under his leadership, Microsoft took early and decisive steps to move its workforce to remote operations. Nadella focused on empathetic leadership, acknowledging the challenges faced by employees, from remote work fatigue to mental health concerns. He emphasized the importance of flexibility, well-being, and encouraged his team to prioritize work-life balance. Microsoft also accelerated its digital offerings, recognizing the increased demand for cloud services and collaboration tools, which was crucial in supporting not only its operations but also those of its customers globally.

Mary Barra - General Motors (GM): Mary Barra, the CEO of General Motors, showcased adaptive leadership by quickly pivoting the company's operations at the onset of the pandemic. GM shifted some of its manufacturing capacity to produce ventilators, demonstrating agility and responsiveness to societal needs. Barra emphasized transparent communication and regularly updated employees on company plans and safety measures, helping to alleviate anxiety and uncertainty. She also championed flexibility, allowing employees to work remotely where possible, and focused on maintaining team cohesion through virtual engagements.

Indra Nooyi - Former CEO of PepsiCo: Although Indra Nooyi stepped down as CEO before the pandemic, her leadership style during her tenure at PepsiCo offers valuable insights into leading during crises. Known for her empathetic and inclusive leadership, Nooyi has been vocal about the importance of understanding employees' needs and challenges during the pandemic. Her advocacy for work-life balance, mental health, and employee well-being, as well as her emphasis on adaptive and compassionate leadership, provides a relevant case study for leading in challenging times.

Eric Yuan - Zoom: As the CEO of Zoom, Eric Yuan found himself at the helm of a company that suddenly became integral to global communication during the pandemic. Yuan's focus on rapidly scaling up Zoom's infrastructure to meet surging demand while maintaining service quality was a testament to agile leadership. He also emphasized customer support and security enhancements in response to new challenges, showcasing his adaptability to changing user needs and concerns.

These leaders exemplify how adaptability, empathy, transparent communication, and a focus on innovation and employee well-being are crucial in navigating the complex challenges posed by the pandemic. Their actions and strategies provide valuable lessons and inspiration for leaders globally, demonstrating effective ways to adapt leadership styles in response to a rapidly changing world.

The shift to remote work, accelerated by the COVID-19 pandemic, has fundamentally altered the landscape of employee engagement. In a remote setting, the traditional methods of fostering engagement, such as in-person meetings and office-based interactions, are no longer feasible. This change has prompted leaders to explore new tools and techniques to engage and motivate their teams effectively.

Relationship Between Remote Work and Employee Engagement

Remote work presents both challenges and opportunities for employee engagement. On one hand, the lack of physical presence can lead to feelings of isolation and disconnection among team members. The absence of casual, spontaneous interactions that typically happen in an office setting can impact team cohesion and a sense of belonging. On the other hand, remote work offers flexibility and autonomy, which can be significant motivators and contribute to higher job satisfaction and engagement when managed effectively.

Effective Tools and Techniques for Engaging Remote Teams

1. Digital Communication Platforms: Tools like Slack, Microsoft Teams, and Zoom have become essential in maintaining communication in remote teams. These platforms allow for real-time messaging, video conferencing, and file sharing, keeping team members connected and facilitating collaboration.

2. Project Management Software: Tools such as Asana, Trello, and Monday.com help in organizing tasks, setting deadlines, and tracking progress. They provide transparency in work

processes and keep everyone aligned on project goals and timelines.

3. Virtual Team-Building Activities: Creative online team-building activities, such as virtual coffee breaks, online games, and team challenges, can help foster a sense of community and connection among remote workers.

4. Regular Check-Ins and Virtual Meetings: Scheduled one-on-one and team meetings can help leaders stay connected with their team members, discuss progress, provide feedback, and address any concerns. These meetings can also serve as a platform for recognizing achievements and celebrating milestones, which are key to maintaining morale and motivation.

5. Online Training and Development Programs: Providing opportunities for professional growth through online courses, webinars, and virtual workshops can keep employees engaged and committed to their personal and career development.

6. Employee Recognition Platforms: Utilizing platforms like Bonusly or Kudos can be an effective way to recognize and reward employees' contributions, fostering a culture of appreciation and positive reinforcement.

7. Flexible Scheduling: Allowing team members to have control over their work schedules (where possible) can lead to higher job satisfaction and engagement. It recognizes the diverse personal circumstances and promotes a balance between work and personal life.

8. Mental Health and Wellness Resources: Offering resources such as virtual wellness sessions, access to mental health professionals, or subscriptions to mindfulness apps can be crucial in supporting the overall well-being of remote workers.

The relationship between remote work and employee engagement is nuanced, requiring leaders to employ a combination of tools and techniques to effectively engage their teams. By leveraging digital communication platforms, organizing virtual team-building activities, maintaining regular check-ins, offering professional development opportunities, recognizing employee contributions, and supporting mental health and wellness, leaders can foster a robust and engaging remote work environment.

Creating a supportive and inclusive virtual work culture in the era of remote work is a critical task that goes beyond simply managing work from a distance. The transition from traditional office environments to virtual spaces demands a nuanced approach to foster a sense of belonging, inclusivity, and support among dispersed team members. Without the physical presence and the subtle interactions of face-to-face environments, employees in a virtual setting can easily feel isolated and disconnected. Addressing this requires intentional efforts from leaders to build a culture that bridges these gaps.

Fostering a sense of belonging is crucial. Leaders must ensure that every team member feels they are an integral part of the organization, even in the absence of physical interaction. This involves creating opportunities for regular team meetings and virtual social events that encourage informal interactions and open communication. Celebrating team achievements and acknowledging personal milestones contributes to building a sense of community within the team.

Effective communication in a virtual setting should be inclusive and ensure that all team members, irrespective of their location, role, or time zone, are kept informed and have equal opportunities to contribute. Structuring meetings to allow for equal participation and using collaboration tools for asynchronous communication are ways to achieve this.

The diversity of workstyles and personal needs also takes on greater significance in a virtual environment. Understanding and accommodating individual preferences in communication, work hours, and the need for flexibility, especially for those balancing work with other responsibilities, is key to an inclusive work culture. Providing a variety of work tools and options can help cater to different needs, promoting flexibility and inclusiveness.

Accessibility and equity are vital. Ensuring that virtual workspaces and tools are accessible to all, including those with disabilities, is essential for creating an equitable environment. This may involve providing assistive technologies and designing meetings and content to be accessible to everyone. Given the blurred lines between professional and personal life in remote work, promoting mental health and well-being is more important than ever. This includes providing support resources, encouraging breaks, respecting non-working hours, and normalizing conversations about mental health.

Continued training and development are also important in maintaining employee engagement and growth in a virtual environment. Providing opportunities for virtual training, e-learning, and networking helps in personal and professional development. Regular feedback and recognition in a virtual setting are as important as in a physical office. Leaders should provide constructive feedback through one-on-one virtual meetings and recognize contributions in team calls or through digital platforms.

In the post-COVID landscape of work, characterized by its rapid evolution and unpredictability, building resilience and adaptability within teams has become more important than ever. The ability of a team to withstand and bounce back from challenges, and to adapt to new circumstances, is crucial not just for surviving but for thriving in the face of future uncertainties. Resilience in teams translates to a collective strength that enables them to deal with setbacks, changes, and pressures effectively. This quality is particularly important in today's fast-paced work environment, where disruptions are frequent and change is constant. A resilient team is better equipped to handle such challenges, maintaining productivity and morale even in difficult times. This resilience is fostered through a supportive work culture, where failures are seen as opportunities for learning and growth, and where open communication and mutual support are the norms.

Adaptability, on the other hand, is about the flexibility and willingness of the team to embrace change. In an ever-changing business landscape, the ability to pivot quickly and effectively is a significant competitive advantage. Adaptable teams can respond to changing market conditions, new technologies, and evolving customer needs with agility and creativity. This adaptability is nurtured by encouraging a mindset of continuous learning, fostering a culture of innovation, and being open to new ideas and approaches.

The importance of building these qualities in teams cannot be overstated. Teams that are resilient and adaptable are more likely to be innovative, as they are not afraid to take risks and are open to exploring new avenues. They are also better at problem-solving, as they can approach challenges from various angles and are not deterred by setbacks.

Resilient and adaptable teams contribute to a positive work environment. They tend to have a more optimistic outlook, can manage stress more effectively, and support each other, which enhances overall team performance and well-being. In preparing for future challenges, leaders play a crucial role in cultivating these qualities within their teams. This involves providing the necessary resources and support, setting an example in terms of attitude and behavior, and creating an environment where resilience and adaptability are valued and encouraged.

Empowering employees and investing in their upskilling are critical strategies for fostering sustained motivation and growth in today's dynamic work environment. These approaches have gained even more relevance in the context of the rapid changes and challenges presented by the modern business landscape, including the shift to more remote and digital working conditions.

Empowering Employees

Empowering employees involves giving them the autonomy, resources, and authority to make decisions about their work. This empowerment is rooted in trust and respect, and it acknowledges that employees are capable and motivated to do their best work when they feel a sense of ownership and responsibility. Empowered employees are more likely to be engaged, committed, and motivated, as they feel valued and know that their contributions matter.

The role of leaders in this process is to create an environment where empowerment is not just encouraged but actively facilitated. This involves delegating meaningful responsibilities, providing the necessary tools and resources, and creating a culture where taking initiative is rewarded. Empowerment also means allowing employees to have a voice in decisions that affect their work and the organization, fostering a sense of involvement and belonging.

Upskilling for Growth

Upskilling – the process of teaching employees new and advanced skills – is another key factor in maintaining motivation and promoting growth. The rapid pace of technological advancement and changing industry needs make continuous learning and development essential. By investing in their employees' upskilling, organizations not only enhance their workforce's capabilities but also demonstrate a commitment to their employees' professional growth and career advancement.

Upskilling can take many forms, from formal training and education programs to more informal methods like mentoring, cross-training, and on-the-job learning opportunities. The goal is to keep the skill set of employees relevant and updated, allowing them to stay agile and adaptable in an ever-evolving work environment.

Upskilling contributes to employee motivation by providing them with challenges and opportunities to progress. It helps in building a more competent and confident workforce, which in turn drives innovation and productivity. Employees who feel that their employer is invested in their growth are more likely to be engaged and committed to the organization.

This chapter has provided a comprehensive exploration of the various adaptations and strategies that leaders have employed to effectively navigate the challenges and opportunities presented by the shift to remote and hybrid work environments, post-COVID-19. Central to this discussion has been the recognition of how the pandemic has reshaped the workplace, altering traditional notions of employee engagement, motivation, and leadership.

A key insight is the evolution of communication strategies in remote settings. Leaders have had to become more intentional and innovative in their communication to ensure clarity and maintain connections with their teams. This has involved leveraging digital tools to facilitate seamless and frequent interactions, thus overcoming the barriers of physical distance. The chapter also highlighted the importance of building team cohesion in a virtual environment. Leaders have found creative ways to foster a sense of community and belonging among remote team members. This has been crucial in maintaining team morale and engagement in the absence of face-to-face interactions.

Performance management in remote settings has seen a significant shift from oversight-based methods to a focus on outcomes and results. Leaders have adapted by setting clear goals, providing regular feedback, and utilizing technology to track and support team progress.

The role of empathy has been underscored as a vital leadership quality in these times. Leaders have had to be more attuned to the emotional and psychological needs of their team members, showing understanding and support for the challenges posed by remote work.

We have described the necessity of fostering resilience and adaptability within teams. In an ever-changing business landscape, these qualities are essential for teams to effectively handle challenges and embrace change. Empowering employees and investing in their upskilling emerged as key strategies for sustaining motivation and growth. Empowerment has been about giving employees the autonomy to make decisions and take ownership of their work, while upskilling has focused on providing continuous learning opportunities to keep pace with evolving industry demands.

The chapter has provided valuable insights and strategies for leaders to effectively manage and motivate their teams in the new, post-pandemic work environment. These include enhanced communication, fostering team cohesion, adapting performance management techniques, demonstrating empathy, building resilience and adaptability, empowering employees, and focusing on upskilling. These approaches collectively offer a roadmap for leaders to navigate the challenges of remote and hybrid work settings, ensuring team success and organizational growth.

As we transition from the insights and strategies discussed in the current chapter, the next chapter promises to delve deeper into the evolving dynamics of team collaboration and innovation in the post-pandemic era. Building upon the concepts of motivation and leadership, this upcoming chapter will explore how these foundational elements play a crucial role in fostering an environment conducive to collaboration and driving innovation within teams.

The pandemic has not only transformed how teams operate but also how they collaborate and innovate. In the forthcoming chapter, we will examine the challenges and opportunities that remote and hybrid work models present for team collaboration. We will explore how the motivational strategies and leadership adaptations discussed previously can be leveraged to enhance team synergy and creativity, even when team members are not physically co-located.

We will also delve into the dynamics of fostering a culture of innovation in this new environment. Innovation, in today's context, is not just about technological advancements but also about finding new ways of working, problem-solving, and creating value. The role of leadership in nurturing an innovative mindset and encouraging experimentation and risk-taking will be a key focus.

The next chapter will also discuss practical approaches to facilitate effective collaboration among diverse and dispersed teams. It will explore how technology, communication, and organizational culture intersect to create an environment where ideas can be freely exchanged, and collaborative efforts can lead to impactful innovations.

2. Team Dynamics, Innovation, and Remote Work

The advent of remote and hybrid work models, significantly accelerated by the COVID-19 pandemic, has brought about a fundamental change in team dynamics. As we venture into this chapter, it is essential to set the scene by understanding how these shifts have reshaped the way teams interact, collaborate, and drive innovation.

With the transition to remote and hybrid work, the traditional office environment – a space that fostered spontaneous interactions, face-to-face meetings, and a sense of physical community – has been transformed. Teams are now navigating a landscape where communication is mediated through screens, and collaboration happens across digital platforms. The absence of physical presence has necessitated a rethinking of how team cohesion is maintained, how trust is built, and how a shared sense of purpose is cultivated.

In this new context, the dynamics of teamwork have evolved. The ease of walking over to a colleague's desk for a quick discussion has been replaced by scheduled video calls and asynchronous communication via emails and messaging apps. This shift has both its challenges and benefits. While it can lead to increased flexibility and autonomy, it also poses the risk of isolation, miscommunication, and a potential dip in team morale and camaraderie.

The hybrid model, where some team members work remotely while others are office-based, presents its own set of dynamics. Ensuring inclusivity, fairness, and effective collaboration in such a setup requires thoughtful strategies and an understanding of the unique challenges and opportunities it presents.

This chapter aims to explore these new dynamics in-depth. It will examine how leaders can adapt their approaches to foster strong, cohesive teams in a remote or hybrid setting. We will look into strategies that facilitate effective communication, ensure equitable participation, and maintain a sense of team unity and shared purpose. We will explore this aspect of innovation in remote and hybrid teams. The chapter will explore how these new work models can be leveraged to foster creativity and innovation, and what leaders can do to encourage an environment where innovative ideas are nurtured and brought to fruition.

Remote hiring, a necessity in today's environment, poses its unique challenges. Without the traditional face-to-face interviews, gauging a candidate's full potential and fit within the team becomes a more nuanced task. Assessing not just their technical abilities but also their adaptability to a remote work culture is crucial. The onboarding process, key to integrating new hires into existing teams, also requires careful consideration to ensure it's as effective virtually as it is in person. Once the team is assembled, the challenge shifts to maintaining cohesion without the natural, informal interactions that occur in a physical office. The absence of spontaneous conversations by the water cooler means leaders must find alternative ways to foster these interactions in the digital realm. This effort often requires more structured planning and a proactive approach to encourage regular and effective communication, thereby promoting a sense of belonging among team members.

The virtual workspace, while opening doors to a geographically diverse workforce, also brings the challenge of ensuring diversity and inclusion. Managing a team that spans different time zones, cultures, and backgrounds demands a heightened awareness of inclusivity. This includes being mindful of scheduling, respecting cultural differences, and ensuring equitable participation in virtual meetings.

Communication in a virtual environment, devoid of non-verbal cues, can be prone to misunderstandings. The reliance on technology for interaction can sometimes lead to a lack of clarity and connection, making effective communication a cornerstone of successful remote team management. Building trust among team members who might never meet in person is another critical aspect. In a remote setting, trust is developed through consistent and transparent interactions, underscoring the importance of reliability and open communication.

Navigating these challenges requires leaders to be adaptive, empathetic, and forward-thinking. The virtual environment demands an innovative approach to leadership, one that recognizes and addresses the unique needs of a dispersed team. By employing effective strategies to foster communication, trust, and a sense of community, leaders can ensure their teams remain cohesive and productive, regardless of the physical distance that separates them.

Here are some strategies that can help leaders build strong, cohesive, and efficient remote teams:

Structured and Transparent Communication

Establish clear communication channels and protocols. Use a mix of synchronous (e.g., video calls, real-time chats) and asynchronous (e.g., emails, recorded video messages) communication tools to cater to different needs and time zones. Regular team meetings and one-on-one check-ins can help ensure that everyone is on the same page. Transparency in communication, where team members are kept informed about company updates, project progress, and changes, is crucial.

Fostering Trust

Trust in remote teams is built on reliability and consistency. Encourage team members to be dependable in their commitments and transparent in their capabilities and bandwidth. As a leader, model this behavior by being open about challenges and responsive to team needs. Trust also comes from demonstrating empathy and understanding towards individual circumstances, which can vary widely in a remote setting.

Cultivating a Sense of Community

Create opportunities for informal interactions and socializing, which are essential for building a sense of community. Virtual coffee breaks, online team-building exercises, or casual group chats can provide spaces for team members to connect on a personal level. Celebrating achievements and milestones, both work-related and personal, can also foster a sense of belonging and team spirit.

Effective Team Structures and Compositions

In a remote environment, it's important to structure teams in a way that maximizes collaboration and efficiency. This might involve creating smaller sub-teams or pairs for specific projects to streamline communication and accountability. Consider the diverse skills and strengths of team members when forming these groups, aiming for a balance that complements and enhances the team's overall capabilities.

Clear Roles and Responsibilities

Clearly define roles, responsibilities, and expectations for each team member. This clarity helps prevent overlaps and gaps in the team's work, ensuring that everyone understands their contribution to the team's goals. Regularly reviewing and updating these roles and responsibilities as projects evolve can also help keep the team aligned and focused.

Leveraging Technology Effectively

Utilize appropriate technology tools not just for communication and project management, but also for building team cohesion. Tools like digital whiteboards for brainstorming, project management software for tracking progress, and platforms for informal social interactions can enhance both productivity and team dynamics.

Encouraging Autonomy and Flexibility

Empower team members with the autonomy to manage their tasks and schedules. This shows trust and respect for their ability to work independently, which is crucial in a remote setting. Flexibility, particularly in accommodating different time zones and work-life balance needs, is also key.

Promoting Continuous Learning and Development

Encourage and facilitate ongoing learning and skill development. This can include virtual training sessions, online courses, and regular knowledge-sharing meetings within the team. Continuous learning helps keep the team up-to-date and adaptable to new challenges and technologies.

By implementing these strategies, leaders can effectively address the challenges of remote work, fostering an environment where communication, trust, community, and efficiency thrive. This approach not only enhances the team's current performance but also positions it for long-term success in an increasingly remote-oriented work world.

The shift to remote work, while presenting its challenges, also opens up a wealth of unique opportunities, particularly in terms of accessing global talent and embracing varied perspectives. This new landscape of work has essentially redefined the boundaries of the traditional workplace, offering potential benefits that were less feasible in a conventional office setting.

One of the most significant advantages of remote teams is the access to a global talent pool. With geographical constraints no longer a barrier, organizations can recruit the best candidates from around the world, irrespective of their location. This access to a broader talent pool not only enhances the quality of recruitment but also brings in diverse skill sets that might be scarce in the local market. It allows companies to find the exact skill sets and expertise they need, going beyond the limitations of their immediate geographic location.

The diversity that comes with global teams extends beyond just professional skills. It encompasses a range of cultural, linguistic, and social perspectives, enriching the team's collective knowledge and experience. This diversity can lead to more creative and innovative problem-solving as different viewpoints collide. Teams that comprise members from various backgrounds are often better equipped to understand and cater to a global customer base, making the organization more competitive in a global market.

Remote teams also offer flexibility, which can lead to increased productivity and job satisfaction. Team members can work in settings that they find most comfortable and at times that suit them best, provided they can coordinate effectively with the rest of the team. This flexibility can result in higher motivation levels, as employees are able to balance their work with personal commitments more effectively.

Remote work can lead to cost savings for both employees and employers. Employees save on commuting time and expenses, while employers can reduce costs associated with maintaining physical office spaces. These savings can then be redirected to other areas of the business or towards employee development programs. The virtual nature of remote work encourages the adoption of advanced technology and digital tools. This not only streamlines workflows but also ensures that the organization stays at the forefront of technological advancements. The necessity to adapt to remote work can accelerate digital transformation, driving efficiency and innovation.

Illustrating with real-world examples, several organizations have successfully navigated the challenges of remote work, creating effective team compositions that have driven productivity, innovation, and employee satisfaction. These case studies offer insights into practical applications of the strategies for managing remote teams.

GitHub: Embracing an All-Remote Workforce

GitHub, a platform for software development, is a leading example of a company that has successfully embraced an all-remote workforce. Even before the pandemic, GitHub had a significant portion of its employees working remotely. They have leveraged tools like Slack, Zoom, and of course, their own GitHub platform, to ensure seamless collaboration. GitHub's success lies in its robust remote work culture, which includes clear documentation, asynchronous communication, and a strong emphasis on work-life balance. The company also regularly organizes online social events and fosters an inclusive culture where every employee, regardless of location, feels valued.

Buffer: Transparent and Asynchronous Communication

Buffer, a social media management tool company, operates with a fully remote team spread across multiple time zones. Buffer is known for its transparent company culture, which extends to its remote work practices. The company relies heavily on asynchronous communication to keep team members connected without requiring them to be online at the same time. This approach respects individual work schedules and promotes a healthy work-life balance. Buffer also emphasizes regular team retreats (virtual during the pandemic) to build team cohesion and ensure alignment with company values and goals.

Zapier: Fostering a Remote-First Culture

Zapier, a web automation app, has been a remote-first company since its inception. Their success with a fully distributed team is attributed to several key practices. These include over-communication, where clarity and frequency of communication are prioritized, and a strong emphasis on documentation, ensuring that information is accessible to all team members. Zapier also focuses on hiring individuals who thrive in a self-motivated and autonomous environment, aligning their team composition with the demands of remote work.

Automattic: Leveraging Blogs for Communication

Automattic, the company behind WordPress.com, operates with a 100% remote workforce. They utilize a unique system for internal communication, where much of the company dialogue and updates occur on internal blogs, organized into different streams for various teams and projects. This system promotes transparency and keeps information flowing effectively among team members. Automattic's approach demonstrates how non-traditional communication methods can be successfully leveraged in a remote setting.

These companies exemplify successful remote team compositions, each employing a distinct blend of communication strategies, cultural practices, and technological tools to build a productive and cohesive remote work environment. Their experiences provide valuable lessons for other organizations looking to optimize their remote work models.

Communication in Remote Teams

One of the primary challenges in remote settings is bridging the physical distance between team members. This distance, if not proactively managed through regular and intentional communication, can lead to a sense of isolation and disconnection. Effective communication in this context serves as a vital link, keeping the team informed and engaged, ensuring everyone is on the same page regarding goals and projects, and maintaining a sense of team unity.

The absence of face-to-face interactions, with their accompanying non-verbal cues, increases the risk of misunderstandings in a remote environment. To counter this, communication must be clear, concise, and frequent. This clarity is not just about how messages are conveyed, but also about ensuring they are understood as intended, often necessitating follow-up or feedback mechanisms to confirm comprehension.

Creating an inclusive environment through communication is especially important in remote teams, which often feature diverse members across different time zones, cultures, and languages.

Effective communication practices in such teams need to be inclusive and considerate of these differences, whether it's scheduling meetings at times that suit everyone, using language that is clear and simple, or encouraging participation from all members.

Trust and transparency are foundational to team cohesion, and in remote settings, these are built through transparent and consistent communication. Leaders play a pivotal role in this regard; by communicating openly and regularly, they set a precedent for the rest of the team, fostering a culture of trust. Effective communication is crucial for collaboration and creativity in remote teams. While digital tools can facilitate collaborative sessions, the quality and effectiveness of communication during these interactions are what truly drive creativity and problem-solving.

Maintaining team morale and engagement in a remote setup heavily relies on communication. Recognizing achievements, celebrating milestones, and engaging in informal conversations are all part of creating a virtual workplace that is vibrant and supportive, not just focused on tasks. Communication acts as the lifeline of remote teams, playing a crucial role in bridging distances, ensuring clarity, fostering inclusivity, building trust, encouraging collaboration, and maintaining morale. Tailoring communication practices to the unique needs of a remote team is essential for sustaining healthy team dynamics and cohesion in a virtual work environment.

Effective communication in remote teams is crucial for maintaining productivity, cohesion, and morale. Leveraging technology appropriately and establishing clear communication protocols are key aspects of achieving this. Here are some practical pieces of advice on effective communication methods for remote teams:

1. Choose the Right Communication Tools: Utilize a range of communication tools and platforms that best suit the needs of the team. This can include video conferencing tools like Zoom

or Microsoft Teams for face-to-face meetings, instant messaging platforms like Slack for quick, informal chats, and email for more formal or detailed communications. It's important to use these tools judiciously – for instance, not every communication requires a video call, and some discussions may be more efficiently handled via messaging or email.

2. Establish Clear Communication Protocols: Develop guidelines on how different communication tools should be used. This includes defining what types of communication are best suited for each platform, setting expectations for response times, and establishing etiquette for virtual meetings (e.g., muting when not speaking, being on camera).

3. Regular Check-Ins and Meetings: Schedule regular team meetings and one-on-one check-ins to ensure ongoing, open communication. This helps in aligning team goals, tracking progress, and addressing any issues or concerns. It also provides a regular forum for team members to connect and engage with each other.

4. Foster Open and Inclusive Communication: Encourage a culture where team members feel comfortable sharing their ideas, feedback, and concerns. In virtual meetings, make a conscious effort to involve all participants, giving everyone a chance to speak. Being mindful of different time zones and cultural nuances is also important to ensure inclusivity.

5. Leverage Collaborative Tools: Use project management and collaboration tools like Asana, Trello, or Monday.com to keep track of tasks, deadlines, and progress. These tools offer transparency and can reduce the need for excessive meetings or emails.

6. Encourage Informal Interactions: Create opportunities for informal interactions and socializing, which are vital for team bonding and can often lead to creative ideas and solutions.

This can include virtual coffee breaks, team lunches over video chat, or online team-building activities.

7. Provide Training on Communication Tools: Ensure that all team members are comfortable using the chosen communication and collaboration tools. Offering training or resources can help team members effectively utilize these tools.

8. Asynchronous Communication: Embrace asynchronous communication, especially if the team is spread across different time zones. This means not all communications need immediate responses, allowing team members to work and reply when it's most convenient for them.

9. Clarity and Conciseness: Encourage clarity and conciseness in all forms of communication. In a remote setting, it's even more important to be clear and direct to avoid misunderstandings.

10. Feedback Mechanisms: Implement mechanisms for regular feedback. This could be through surveys, suggestion boxes, or regular check-ins, to continually improve communication strategies.

By integrating these practices into their communication approach, leaders can ensure that their remote teams stay connected, aligned, and productive, regardless of their physical locations.

Fostering Innovation Remotely

Fostering innovation in dispersed teams presents specific challenges, notably the reduction in spontaneous interactions which often spark creative ideas in traditional office settings. The physical separation of team members in a remote environment means that opportunities for casual, impromptu conversations – by the water cooler, in the hallway, or during lunch breaks – are significantly diminished. These casual interactions have traditionally played a crucial role in exchanging ideas and perspectives, thereby fostering an environment ripe for innovation. Another challenge is ensuring that all team members, regardless of their location, feel equally involved and heard. In a dispersed team, there can be a tendency for remote members to feel disconnected from the main group, especially if some team members are co-located while others are not. This can lead to a situation where ideas and contributions are unevenly distributed, hindering the collaborative spirit necessary for innovation.

Maintaining a consistent level of engagement and motivation across the team is also more complex in a remote setting. Without the energy and dynamism of a shared physical workspace, keeping team members inspired and creatively stimulated requires deliberate effort and strategy. The absence of physical whiteboards, shared spaces, and face-to-face brainstorming sessions can pose a barrier to visual and collaborative ideation processes. While digital tools offer alternatives, they may not fully replicate the spontaneity and fluidity of in-person brainstorming.

To address these challenges, leaders need to create structured opportunities for interaction and idea-sharing. This can include regular brainstorming sessions, innovation-focused meetings, and virtual collaboration spaces where team members can spontaneously share and develop ideas. Encouraging a culture where all ideas are welcomed and valued, regardless of how unformed or unconventional they might be, can also help in fostering innovation. Leaders must also ensure that communication channels are open and accessible to all team members, fostering an inclusive environment where every voice can be heard. Regular check-ins, feedback sessions, and an emphasis on clear, open communication can help in maintaining engagement and motivation across dispersed teams.

Technology also plays a crucial role in overcoming these challenges. Utilizing digital collaboration tools effectively can facilitate brainstorming and idea-sharing in a virtual environment. Tools like digital whiteboards, mind-mapping software, and online ideation platforms can help replicate some of the collaborative energy of physical spaces.

Encouraging and maintaining creativity and innovation in remote teams, despite the inherent challenges, can be achieved through concrete and actionable strategies. These strategies are designed to foster an environment where ideas can flourish, collaboration is encouraged, and every team member feels empowered to contribute creatively.

1. Structured Virtual Brainstorming Sessions: Regularly schedule virtual brainstorming sessions where team members can share and build on each other's ideas. Use digital tools like virtual whiteboards or brainstorming apps to facilitate these sessions. Structure them with clear objectives but allow for free-flowing, open-ended discussions to encourage creative thinking.

2. Idea-Sharing Platforms: Implement an online platform or dedicated space where team members can post ideas, inspirations, or interesting finds at any time. This can be a channel on a communication platform like Slack or a section in a project management tool like Asana. It serves as a digital equivalent of a physical idea board and encourages continuous sharing of ideas.

3. Regular Innovation Challenges: Organize regular challenges or hackathons where team members can work on innovative projects outside of their regular responsibilities. These can be individual or team-based projects and should encourage thinking outside the box. Offer recognition or rewards for the best ideas or solutions.

4. Encourage Cross-Functional Collaboration: Create opportunities for team members from different functions or departments to collaborate on projects. This cross-pollination of skills and perspectives can lead to more innovative solutions and ideas.

5. Flexible Scheduling for Creative Work: Recognize that creativity can't always be scheduled. Allow flexibility in work

hours for team members to work when they feel most creative or inspired, respecting individual peaks in creativity.

6. Professional Development Opportunities: Offer opportunities for team members to learn and develop new skills. This can be through online courses, webinars, or virtual workshops. Expanding skill sets can inspire new ideas and approaches.

7. Foster a Culture of Openness and Experimentation: Encourage a team culture where experimentation is welcomed, and failure is viewed as a learning opportunity. Ensure that team members feel safe and supported to take risks and try out new ideas.

8. Regular Feedback and Recognition: Provide regular feedback on creative initiatives and recognize innovative contributions. Acknowledgement and appreciation of creative efforts can significantly boost motivation and encourage further innovation.

9. Virtual Social Interactions: Facilitate virtual social interactions to mimic informal office interactions where a lot of creative ideas are often exchanged. This could be through virtual coffee breaks, casual hangout sessions, or interest-based groups.

The lack of physical interaction in remote teams has necessitated the use of digital solutions to bridge the gap, facilitating brainstorming, project development, and seamless communication.

Virtual whiteboard tools have become indispensable for remote teams. Platforms like Miro or Mural offer a digital canvas where team members can collaboratively brainstorm, sketch out ideas, and visually map out concepts, replicating the experience of a physical whiteboard session. These tools support real-time collaboration and are excellent for facilitating creative sessions, organizing thoughts, and developing ideas in a visually engaging way.

Project management software, such as Asana, Trello, or Monday.com, also plays a key role in remote innovation. These platforms help in organizing ideas, tracking progress on innovative projects, and managing tasks and timelines. They provide a central hub where all team members can see the big picture, understand their individual roles, and how their work contributes to the broader project goals.

For communication, platforms like Slack and Microsoft Teams have become the backbone of remote team interactions. Beyond just text messaging, these platforms support file sharing, video calls, and integration with other tools, making them a one-stop shop for team communication and collaboration. They also allow for the creation of dedicated channels for specific projects or topics, keeping conversations focused and organized. Video conferencing tools such as Zoom or Google Meet are critical for face-to-face interaction, which is vital for maintaining team connections and fostering a collaborative spirit. These tools are essential for conducting regular team meetings, one-on-one check-ins, and brainstorming sessions, helping to maintain a personal connection despite the physical distance.

Cloud storage and collaboration services like Google Drive, Dropbox, or OneDrive are essential for sharing and working on documents collaboratively. They allow team members to access, edit, and comment on documents, spreadsheets, or presentations in real-time, ensuring that everyone is working with the most up-to-date information.

Innovation management software, like Planbox or Brightidea, can also be valuable for remote teams. These platforms are designed to manage the innovation process from idea generation to implementation, providing tools for submitting ideas, evaluating them, and tracking their progress towards realization. Creativity and mind-mapping software like MindMeister or XMind offer a way for team members to visually organize their thoughts and ideas. These tools are particularly useful in the early stages of a project or brainstorming session, helping to spark creative thinking and capture ideas in a structured way.

Incorporating these technological tools and platforms into remote work practices can significantly enhance the team's ability to innovate and collaborate effectively. They not only compensate for the lack of physical interaction but also bring unique capabilities that can augment the creative process.

Several remote teams across various industries have successfully fostered innovation by leveraging technology and effective remote work practices. Their experiences provide insightful case studies on how to drive creativity and progress in a virtual setting.

GitLab's Remote-First Success

GitLab, the open-source DevOps platform, is renowned for its all-remote workforce and has been a paragon of remote innovation even before the pandemic. With over 1,300 employees working remotely from more than 65 countries, GitLab has successfully created a highly transparent work environment. They utilize a range of digital tools for collaboration and emphasize asynchronous communication, which allows for flexibility and productivity across different time zones. GitLab's culture of open-source contribution and continuous feedback encourages innovation among its team members, resulting in a robust, community-driven product development process.

Buffer's Transparent Remote Work Culture

Buffer, a social media management platform, operates with a fully remote team and is known for its strong culture of transparency and communication. Buffer has successfully leveraged tools like Trello and Zoom to facilitate team collaboration and innovation. Their regular 'Buffer Retreats', though virtual during the pandemic, have been instrumental in fostering team bonding and brainstorming new ideas. Despite the geographical dispersion of its team, Buffer maintains a high level of innovation and agility in its product development, attributed to its emphasis on open communication and employee empowerment.

Zapier's Efficient Remote Operations

Zapier, an automation tool that connects different apps and services, runs on a 100% remote model. The company stands out for its efficient remote operations and its ability to foster a culture of innovation among its workforce. Zapier uses a combination of Slack, GitHub, and Zoom to keep its team members connected and collaborative. The company also implements regular 'hack weeks' where employees can work on creative projects outside their regular scope, encouraging innovation and new ideas.

Maintaining Team Morale and Engagement

Keeping up team morale and engagement is crucial in any work environment, but it takes on added significance in a remote context. The physical separation and lack of in-person interaction that characterizes remote work can lead to feelings of isolation and disconnection among team members. This can, in turn, impact their engagement, productivity, and overall job satisfaction. Hence, maintaining high morale and engagement is vital for the health and success of remote teams.

Morale is closely tied to motivation. When team members feel positive and valued, they are more likely to be motivated and committed to their work. High morale leads to a more energized and enthusiastic workforce, which can boost productivity and creativity. In a remote setting, where the usual office environment cues and motivations are absent, keeping morale high requires more deliberate effort and strategy from leaders.

Engagement in a remote setting is key to ensuring that team members feel connected to their work and the organization. Remote work can sometimes make individuals feel like they're working in a vacuum, leading to a sense of detachment from the broader goals and mission of the organization. Ensuring that employees remain engaged with their work, understanding how their contributions fit into the bigger picture, is essential for maintaining a cohesive and effective team.

High morale and engagement are crucial for team cohesion and a sense of belonging. Remote teams lack the natural bonding that occurs in a physical workspace, which can impact team dynamics and collaboration. Building a sense of community and a collaborative team culture is important for remote teams, and this is heavily influenced by the overall morale and engagement of its members.

Keeping up morale and engagement is vital for employee retention. The remote work environment, while offering flexibility, can also lead to higher turnover if team members feel disconnected, undervalued, or unsupported. Fostering a positive and engaging remote work environment can help in retaining talent and reducing the costs and disruptions associated with high turnover rates.

Maintaining morale and engagement in a remote context is not just about the well-being of employees, but also about the productivity, cohesion, and long-term sustainability of the team. Leaders play a critical role in this process, needing to employ various strategies and tools to ensure their remote teams remain motivated, engaged, and connected.

Keeping remote teams engaged and motivated requires thoughtful strategies and activities that cater to the unique challenges of a virtual work environment. Leaders can adopt a variety of approaches to ensure their teams remain productive, connected, and motivated:

1. Regular Virtual Meetings: Hold regular team meetings and one-on-one check-ins to maintain open lines of communication. Use these meetings not just for work-related updates but also for personal check-ins, helping to build rapport and a sense of community within the team.

2. Recognition and Rewards: Recognize and celebrate successes, both big and small. Acknowledging individual and team achievements can boost morale and motivation. This could be through shout-outs during meetings, virtual awards, or even small rewards.

3. Team Building Activities: Organize virtual team-building activities to foster camaraderie and teamwork. This could include online games, virtual happy hours, or fun challenges that team members can participate in.

4. Flexible Work Arrangements: Recognize the diverse personal circumstances of remote workers and offer flexible working arrangements. Flexibility can greatly enhance job satisfaction and motivation.

5. Professional Development Opportunities: Encourage and facilitate opportunities for professional growth. This could include access to online courses, webinars, virtual conferences, or internal training sessions.

6. Transparent Communication: Maintain transparency in communication regarding company news, updates, and changes. Keeping team members in the loop fosters trust and a sense of security.

7. Encourage Breaks and Downtime: Promote a healthy work-life balance by encouraging regular breaks, downtime, and vacations. This helps prevent burnout and keeps the team refreshed and motivated.

8. Creating a Virtual Open Door Policy: Make it known that team members can reach out to leaders with concerns, ideas, or for support. An open-door policy in a virtual environment promotes trust and open communication.

9. Collaborative Project Management Tools: Utilize project management tools that allow for collaboration and transparency in workflows. Tools like Asana, Trello, or Monday.com can help keep everyone aligned and engaged with their tasks.

10. Virtual Mentorship and Buddy Systems: Implement mentorship programs or buddy systems for new hires or for career development. This can help in building relationships

within the team and provide support for personal and professional growth.

11. Health and Wellness Initiatives: Offer programs or resources focused on mental health and physical well-being, such as virtual fitness classes, meditation sessions, or access to counseling services.

12. Feedback Mechanisms: Regularly solicit feedback from team members on their work experience and suggestions for improvement. This can be through surveys, suggestion boxes, or during meetings.

By implementing these strategies, leaders can create a remote work environment that is not only productive but also supportive, engaging, and motivating for all team members.

In a remote work environment, measuring team morale and engagement can be challenging, yet it's crucial for maintaining a healthy and productive team. Various tools and methods are available to help leaders gauge the pulse of their remote teams effectively.

Surveys are a popular tool for measuring team morale and engagement. Platforms like SurveyMonkey or Google Forms can be used to create anonymous surveys where team members can provide feedback on their work experience, job satisfaction, and any concerns they might have. Regular surveys can track changes in morale over time and provide insights into areas needing improvement.

Pulse surveys, shorter and more frequent than traditional surveys, are another effective method. Tools like Officevibe or TinyPulse offer pulse survey functionalities that can quickly assess how team members are feeling, allowing leaders to address issues promptly.

Engagement software platforms provide a comprehensive solution for measuring and improving team engagement and morale. Platforms like Qualtrics Employee Experience or Culture Amp offer tools for surveying, gathering feedback, and analyzing data to identify trends and areas of improvement.

Virtual one-on-one meetings are a direct and personal method for gauging team morale. These meetings give team members an opportunity to discuss any issues privately and provide leaders with valuable insights into individual well-being and engagement. Performance metrics, while primarily focused on output, can also provide indirect indicators of team morale. A sudden drop in productivity or quality of work might signal underlying issues related to morale or engagement.

Online communication tools can offer anecdotal evidence of team morale. The tone and frequency of messages on platforms like Slack or Microsoft Teams can give leaders a sense of the team's mood and engagement. Social interaction platforms or virtual team-building events can also be a source of insights. How team members interact during these events, their level of participation, and the nature of their interactions can provide clues about the team's overall morale.

Feedback and suggestion tools embedded within project management software or intranets allow team members to share their thoughts and suggestions anonymously. This can be a valuable source of information for understanding team sentiment. Mental health and wellness apps or programs can provide insights into the overall well-being of the team, which is closely related to morale. Programs like Headspace or Calm, if offered as part of employee benefits, can include anonymous aggregate reporting on usage and engagement. By utilizing these tools and methods, leaders can effectively measure and track the morale and engagement of their remote teams. This understanding is crucial for taking proactive steps to address issues and maintain a positive and productive work environment.

Building a Culture of Trust and Collaboration

Trust is a fundamental component of successful remote teams, playing an even more critical role in virtual settings than in traditional office environments. In the absence of regular, face-to-face interactions, trust becomes the foundation on which effective communication, collaboration, and overall team dynamics are built.

In remote teams, trust is crucial for fostering a sense of security and reliability among team members. When team members trust each other, they are more open in their communication, willing to share ideas, and comfortable expressing concerns or challenges. This openness is vital for collaboration and innovation, as it encourages a free exchange of ideas and constructive feedback.

Trust empowers team members to work autonomously. Remote work often requires a degree of flexibility and self-management that is not as prevalent in office settings. Trusting team members to manage their workload, make decisions, and meet deadlines without constant supervision is key to maintaining productivity and motivation in a remote environment.

For leaders, building and maintaining trust in a remote team involves consistent and transparent communication, showing empathy and understanding towards team members' individual circumstances, and following through on commitments and promises. It also means providing support and resources necessary for team members to perform their roles effectively. Trust in remote teams mitigates the challenges posed by physical distance. It helps in overcoming the potential feelings of isolation and disconnection, contributing to a stronger team culture and better overall team performance.

Trust acts as the glue that holds remote teams together. It is essential for creating a positive and supportive work environment where team members feel valued, connected, and committed to shared goals. Building and sustaining trust in a virtual team setting requires deliberate effort and consistent practice but is crucial for the long-term success and cohesion of the team.

Building and maintaining a culture of collaboration in remote teams involves a strategic approach that takes into account the unique challenges of virtual work environments. The key lies in fostering an atmosphere where team members feel connected, valued, and motivated to work together, despite the physical distance.

Creating a strong foundation for collaboration starts with effective and inclusive communication. Establishing clear communication channels and regular check-ins helps ensure that all team members are on the same page. It's important to encourage open dialogue where team members can share ideas, concerns, and feedback freely. This openness not only promotes transparency but also helps in building mutual trust.

Encouraging active participation is crucial. In virtual meetings, for instance, make a conscious effort to involve every team member, giving them a platform to contribute. This could mean rotating meeting facilitation roles or setting aside time for each member to share updates and ideas. Such practices ensure that everyone's voice is heard and valued. Leveraging technology effectively plays a significant role in fostering collaboration. Utilize collaboration tools and project management software that enable team members to work together efficiently, regardless of their location. These tools should facilitate sharing of documents, tracking progress, and coordinating tasks seamlessly.

Building a sense of community and team spirit is also important. This can be achieved through virtual team-building activities, casual catch-ups, or interest-based groups within the team. Such initiatives help in creating bonds beyond work-related tasks, which is important for team cohesion.

Setting clear goals and expectations is another key aspect. When team members understand their roles and how their work contributes to the broader objectives, they are more likely to collaborate effectively. Regularly revisiting these goals and adapting them as needed keeps the team aligned and focused. Fostering a culture of learning and development helps in maintaining a collaborative environment. Encouraging team members to share knowledge, learn from each other, and engage in joint problem-solving activities can stimulate a collaborative mindset.

Recognizing and celebrating collaborative achievements is vital. Acknowledging the team's efforts and successes in working together reinforces the value of collaboration and encourages continued cooperative behavior. Being mindful of work-life balance is important. Ensuring that team members do not feel overwhelmed or burnt out is key to maintaining a healthy and collaborative team environment.

Fostering a trusting and collaborative remote work environment involves a combination of best practices and techniques tailored to overcome the challenges of distance and virtual interaction. The key is to create a culture where open communication, mutual respect, and team spirit are at the forefront.

Encouraging open and transparent communication is fundamental. Regular team meetings and one-on-one check-ins are essential to keep everyone informed and aligned. It's important to establish a culture where team members feel comfortable sharing their thoughts, challenges, and successes. Leaders should lead by example, being open about their own challenges and encouraging others to share. Building trust among team members is crucial. This can be achieved by consistently meeting commitments and deadlines, being reliable in communication, and showing up for team meetings and discussions. Trust is also fostered when team members feel their contributions are valued and their voices are heard.

Creating opportunities for informal interactions and socializing can significantly enhance team bonding and collaboration. Virtual coffee breaks, team lunches over video chat, or online team-building activities can help team members connect on a personal level, which is vital for building trust and collaboration.

Establishing clear roles and responsibilities while promoting autonomy and empowerment is important. When team members clearly understand their roles and the expectations of them, and feel empowered to make decisions, it fosters a sense of ownership and responsibility, which is key to collaboration. Using collaborative tools and technology effectively can greatly aid in building a collaborative environment. Tools for project management, document sharing, and communication should be used to keep everyone on the same page and facilitate seamless collaboration.

Recognizing and celebrating team achievements and collaborative efforts is also a best practice. This not only motivates the team but also reinforces the value placed on collaboration and collective success.

Encouraging continuous learning and knowledge sharing among team members can foster a culture of collaboration. When team members learn together and from each other, it builds a sense of camaraderie and shared purpose. Leaders need to be attentive to the well-being of their team members. Regularly checking in on their mental and emotional health, especially in a remote setting, is important for maintaining a positive and supportive work environment.

Being adaptable and flexible, especially in terms of work schedules and individual needs, is crucial in a remote setting. Flexibility shows respect for individual circumstances and builds mutual trust. Implementing these best practices and techniques can help create a remote work environment where trust, collaboration, and team spirit thrive, leading to a more engaged, productive, and satisfied team.

The chapter on fostering collaboration and trust in remote teams delved into several key points and strategies essential for the success of virtual work environments. These focused on overcoming the unique challenges posed by remote work to maintain team cohesion, productivity, and a positive work culture.

Open and transparent communication was emphasized as the cornerstone of successful remote teams. Regular team meetings and one-on-one check-ins are vital to keep everyone informed and aligned. Encouraging a culture where team members are comfortable sharing their ideas and challenges helps in building trust and ensures everyone feels heard and valued.

Trust among team members was identified as crucial and can be built through consistency in meeting commitments, reliability in communication, and respect for each other's contributions. Trust is further enhanced by recognizing and valuing the input of all team members and by leaders modeling this behavior. The importance of informal interactions and socializing in a virtual setting was highlighted. Activities like virtual coffee breaks and team lunches foster personal connections and team bonding, essential for a collaborative and supportive work environment. Clear definition of roles and responsibilities, along with empowering team members to make decisions, was noted as important for fostering a sense of ownership and responsibility, which are key to effective collaboration. Utilizing technology effectively for collaboration was discussed, including the use of project management tools, document sharing platforms, and communication software to facilitate seamless teamwork.

Recognizing and celebrating team achievements and collaborative efforts helps in motivating the team and reinforcing the value of working together. Continuous learning and knowledge sharing among team members were suggested as means to foster a collaborative culture, encouraging team members to learn together and from each other.

The well-being of team members was underscored as a priority, with leaders needing to be attentive to the mental and emotional health of their teams, particularly in a remote setting. Adaptability and flexibility were presented as crucial elements, especially regarding work schedules and individual needs, to build mutual trust and respect in a remote team.

As we wrap up our in-depth discussion on trust and collaboration in remote teams, we naturally transition to the next critical theme in the realm of remote work: Organizational Culture and Agile Change Management. This upcoming chapter builds on the foundational concepts of trust and collaboration, delving into how they intricately weave into and influence the broader organizational culture, particularly in the context of managing change.

In the forthcoming chapter, we will explore the dynamics of shaping and sustaining a positive and effective organizational culture in a remote work environment. This includes understanding the nuances of creating a company culture that transcends physical boundaries and fosters a sense of shared values and mission among dispersed teams.

We will dive into the concept of agile change management. In today's fast-paced and ever-evolving business landscape, the ability to adapt and respond swiftly to change is more crucial than ever. We will examine how organizations can adopt agile principles to manage change more effectively, ensuring that they remain resilient and competitive in the face of continuous market and technological shifts.

This chapter will also address the role of leadership in steering organizational culture and change management. We will look at how leaders can act as catalysts for cultivating a culture that embraces change and how they can guide their teams through the uncertainties and opportunities that come with it.

The upcoming chapter on Organizational Culture and Agile Change Management will provide a comprehensive guide on how to embed a culture of agility and resilience within an organization. It will tie in the principles of trust, communication, and collaboration to offer a holistic view of leading and managing in a modern, remote-first work environment.

3. Organizational Culture and Agile Change Management

In today's rapidly evolving business landscape, organizational culture stands as a pivotal element shaping the identity, cohesion, and resilience of companies. Organizational culture refers to the shared values, beliefs, practices, and behaviors that define how work gets done within an organization. It encompasses the collective mindset and ethos of a company, influencing everything from decision-making processes to employee interactions and customer engagement.

The significance of organizational culture in the modern business world cannot be overstated. It acts as a compass that guides the actions and strategies of a company, particularly in times of change and uncertainty. A strong, positive organizational culture fosters a sense of identity and purpose among employees, enhancing engagement, satisfaction, and loyalty. It creates an environment where individuals are motivated to contribute their best, driving productivity and innovation. Moreover, in the context of globalization and technological advancements, organizational culture plays a crucial role in how companies adapt and respond to change. As businesses face new challenges and opportunities, the agility of their culture – the ability to quickly and effectively adapt to new circumstances – becomes a key factor in their success and sustainability.

Agile change management, a concept deeply intertwined with organizational culture, refers to the ability of an organization to swiftly adapt to changes in the external environment. It involves being responsive, flexible, and resilient in the face of market shifts, technological developments, and evolving customer needs. An agile culture is characterized by a willingness to experiment, learn from failures, and continuously improve.

In this chapter, we will explore the intricacies of building and nurturing an organizational culture that is not only strong and cohesive but also agile and adaptive. We will delve into how culture influences an organization's capacity to manage change and the strategies leaders can employ to foster a culture that embraces and thrives on agility and innovation. This exploration will provide valuable insights into creating an organizational environment well-equipped to navigate the complexities and dynamism of the modern business world.

The recent global changes, including the COVID-19 pandemic, technological advancements, and shifting market dynamics, have heightened the need for adaptability and resilience in organizational cultures. These unprecedented shifts have fundamentally altered the business landscape, necessitating a reevaluation of how organizations operate and respond to change.

Adaptability in organizational culture refers to the ability of a company to adjust its strategies, operations, and practices in response to external changes. This agility has become essential in the face of rapid technological advancements and changing consumer behaviors. Organizations that can quickly adapt are better positioned to seize new opportunities, mitigate risks, and maintain competitiveness.

Resilience, on the other hand, is the capacity of an organization to withstand and recover from challenges and setbacks. The recent global events, particularly the pandemic, have underscored the importance of resilience. Organizations with resilient cultures have demonstrated a remarkable ability to navigate the uncertainties brought about by the pandemic, including shifts to remote work, supply chain disruptions, and fluctuating market demands. A culture that values adaptability and resilience encourages a mindset of continuous learning and improvement. It fosters an environment where employees are not afraid to experiment, take calculated risks, and learn from failures. This kind of culture is characterized by flexibility in processes and decision-making, allowing the organization to pivot quickly in response to new information or situations.

A resilient and adaptable organizational culture is crucial for employee morale and engagement. In times of change and uncertainty, a culture that supports and empowers employees contributes to their sense of security and well-being. This, in turn, enhances their engagement and productivity. The recent global changes have also highlighted the need for organizations to be socially responsible and environmentally sustainable. Adaptable and resilient cultures are more likely to integrate these considerations into their business models, recognizing their importance for long-term sustainability.

Adapting Culture for Resilience

The COVID-19 pandemic has acted as a catalyst for significant shifts in organizational culture across the globe. This unprecedented event has forced companies to reevaluate and rapidly adapt their cultural norms, practices, and values, leading to lasting changes in how organizations operate.

One of the most notable shifts has been the widespread adoption of remote work. Prior to the pandemic, remote work was often considered a perk or a limited option for certain roles. However, the pandemic necessitated a swift transition to remote operations, challenging traditional notions of workplace culture. This shift has not only changed where and how people work but also brought about a rethinking of work-life balance, employee autonomy, and flexibility. Organizations have had to cultivate a culture that supports and enables effective remote work, emphasizing trust, communication, and employee well-being.

Another significant cultural shift has been the increased focus on employee health and well-being. The pandemic highlighted the importance of considering employees' physical and mental health as a key component of organizational success. Companies have started to prioritize wellness programs, flexible working hours, and mental health support, recognizing that the well-being of employees directly impacts productivity and engagement.

The pandemic also accelerated digital transformation, pushing organizations to embrace new technologies at an unprecedented pace. This rapid adoption of digital tools and platforms required a cultural shift towards continuous learning and adaptability. Organizations had to foster a culture where employees are encouraged and supported to develop new skills and embrace change.

The pandemic underscored the need for agility and resilience in organizational culture. Companies had to quickly adapt to changing market conditions, supply chain disruptions, and evolving customer needs. Cultures that emphasized quick decision-making, innovation, and adaptability were better positioned to navigate the uncertainties brought about by the pandemic. The crisis also brought to the fore the importance of strong leadership and clear communication. Leaders had to steer their organizations through uncharted waters, requiring a culture of transparency, open communication, and decisive action. The way leaders responded to the crisis significantly impacted organizational culture, employee morale, and public perception.

The pandemic heightened awareness around social responsibility and community support. Many organizations shifted their cultures to be more community-oriented and socially responsible, engaging in initiatives to support pandemic relief efforts or address social inequalities exacerbated by the crisis.

Events like the COVID-19 pandemic have forced substantial shifts in organizational culture, pushing companies to adopt more flexible, digital, employee-centric, and resilient practices. These changes are likely to have a lasting impact on how organizations operate and what they prioritize in their cultures moving forward. Developing an organizational culture that can withstand and adapt to rapid changes and uncertainties is a critical task in today's ever-evolving business landscape. The key lies in fostering certain core attributes and practices within the organizational culture.

A culture of agility is essential. This means cultivating a mindset where change is not only expected but embraced as an opportunity for growth and improvement. Agility in culture allows organizations to pivot quickly in response to changing market dynamics, technological advancements, or unexpected challenges.

Encouraging a mindset of continuous learning and development is also crucial. Organizations that prioritize upskilling and reskilling their workforce create a culture that is better equipped to handle changes. This involves not just formal training programs, but also fostering an environment where learning from day-to-day experiences, experimentation, and even failures is valued.

Building resilience into the organizational fabric is another vital aspect. This involves creating a culture that can bounce back from setbacks. It's about promoting a positive outlook, where challenges are seen as hurdles to overcome rather than insurmountable obstacles. Resilient cultures are characterized by supportive leadership and a strong sense of community among employees, where everyone feels they are in it together.

Transparent and effective communication plays a pivotal role in a culture that can adapt to change. Keeping employees informed about organizational goals, challenges, and changes helps in building trust and ensuring that everyone is aligned and moving in the same direction. Empowering employees is also a key factor. When employees are given the autonomy to make decisions and take ownership of their work, they are more likely to be proactive and innovative. An empowered workforce is more adaptable and can contribute significantly to navigating through uncertainties.

Fostering a collaborative environment is essential for adapting to change. Collaboration leads to a pooling of diverse ideas and perspectives, which is crucial for innovative problem-solving and adapting to new situations. Emphasizing emotional intelligence and empathy in leadership and throughout the organization helps in managing the human aspect of change. Understanding and addressing the concerns and anxieties that change can bring helps in maintaining morale and keeping the team focused and motivated.

Several organizations worldwide have successfully adapted their cultures to enhance resilience, demonstrating the ability to navigate and thrive amidst change and uncertainty.

- Nokia: Once primarily known as a mobile phone manufacturer, Nokia's successful pivot to network and telecommunications technology exemplifies resilience. When the mobile phone industry evolved, Nokia restructured and shifted its focus to network equipment and services, showcasing its ability to adapt to market changes. This resilience was underpinned by a corporate culture that embraced change, encouraged innovation, and fostered a willingness to venture into new business areas.

- Netflix: Originally a DVD rental service, Netflix transformed into a streaming giant and later into content production. This evolution is a testament to its resilient culture. Netflix's ability to foresee and adapt to changes in how people consume entertainment underlines a corporate culture deeply rooted in innovation, adaptability, and customer-centricity.

- Adobe: Known for its creative software, Adobe's shift from boxed software products to a cloud-based subscription model illustrates cultural adaptability. This transition required not only a change in business strategy but also a cultural shift towards continuous product innovation and customer engagement, ensuring the company's sustainability and growth in the digital age.

- IBM: An iconic example of cultural resilience, IBM successfully transitioned from hardware like typewriters and mainframes to software and services. This shift was driven by a culture that valued continuous learning, technological innovation, and adapting to market needs. IBM's ability to reinvent itself multiple times over its long history showcases its resilient and adaptable organizational culture.

These examples demonstrate how fostering a resilient culture, one that values adaptability, continuous learning, and innovation, is essential for organizations to navigate changes successfully and sustain growth over time.

Principles of Agile Change Management

Agile change management refers to a dynamic approach to managing change in organizations, characterized by flexibility, speed, and iterative progress. Unlike traditional change management, which often follows a linear and structured path, agile change management is adaptive, allowing organizations to respond quickly to evolving conditions and feedback.

In the current business environment, marked by rapid technological advancements, shifting market dynamics, and unforeseen events like the COVID-19 pandemic, the relevance of agile change management has become increasingly pronounced. This approach enables organizations to remain competitive and relevant in a landscape where changes occur at an unprecedented pace.

Agile change management is built on the principles of the agile methodology, originally developed for software development. It emphasizes collaboration, customer feedback, and small, rapid iterations. Applying these principles to change management means that changes are implemented in smaller, manageable stages, allowing for quick adjustments based on feedback and changing circumstances.

This approach to change management is particularly relevant now as it allows organizations to test and refine changes before fully implementing them, reducing the risk and cost of failure. It also encourages employee involvement and feedback, which can lead to higher engagement and buy-in for the change. Agile change management supports a culture of continuous improvement, where learning from each stage of change is used to inform future decisions. This is crucial in a business environment where the ability to learn and adapt quickly can provide a significant competitive advantage. It is an approach well-suited to the complexities and uncertainties of the modern business environment. It offers a flexible, responsive, and iterative framework for navigating change, making it an invaluable tool for organizations looking to thrive amidst constant change.

Agile change management, as a strategic approach to handling organizational change, revolves around several key principles that enable organizations to adapt quickly and effectively in a dynamic business environment. These principles include flexibility, responsiveness, and iterative progress, among others.

Flexibility

One of the core tenets of agile change management is flexibility. This principle emphasizes the need for organizations to remain adaptable in their strategies and approaches. Flexibility allows for adjustments to be made during the change process as new information becomes available or circumstances evolve. This contrasts with rigid, plan-driven methods, offering a more dynamic way to manage change.

Responsiveness

Responsiveness in agile change management refers to the ability of an organization to react swiftly to internal and external stimuli. This could include changing market trends, customer feedback, technological advancements, or unexpected challenges. Being responsive means that organizations can quickly realign their change initiatives to meet these evolving demands and capitalize on emerging opportunities.

Iterative Progress

Agile change management advocates for an iterative approach to implementing change. Instead of large, sweeping changes, the process is broken down into smaller, manageable segments. These segments, or iterations, allow for continual assessment and refinement. This approach not only makes the change process more manageable but also allows for faster course corrections and risk mitigation.

Employee Involvement and Collaboration

Agile change management places a strong emphasis on employee involvement. By actively engaging employees in the change process and encouraging collaboration across different levels and departments, organizations can harness diverse perspectives and insights. This involvement also helps in building buy-in and reducing resistance to change.

Continuous Learning and Improvement

An agile approach to change management is underpinned by a commitment to continuous learning and improvement. Each iteration of change is an opportunity to learn, with insights and feedback used to refine future steps. This principle ensures that change management is a dynamic, evolving process, aligned with the organization's learning and growth.

Customer-Centric Focus

Agile methodologies originated in software development with a strong emphasis on customer satisfaction. Applied to change management, this translates into a focus on how changes will impact and benefit the end customer. Keeping the customer perspective in focus ensures that changes are relevant and value-adding.

Transparent Communication

Effective communication is vital in agile change management. Transparency about the change process, its progress, challenges, and successes helps in maintaining trust and clarity among all stakeholders. Open communication channels ensure that feedback is promptly received and addressed.

By integrating these principles, organizations adopting agile change management can navigate change more effectively, making the process a collaborative, flexible, and iterative journey that aligns with the evolving needs of the business and its stakeholders.

Strategies for Implementing Agile Change

Implementing change in an agile manner involves several approaches that emphasize flexibility, responsiveness, and continuous improvement. These approaches are designed to adapt to the fast-paced and often unpredictable business environment. Cross-functional teams are a key element in agile change management. By bringing together individuals with diverse skills and perspectives from various departments, organizations can tackle change from a holistic viewpoint. These teams are empowered to make decisions and act quickly, which is crucial in responding to changing circumstances. The collaborative nature of cross-functional teams also ensures that different aspects of the organization are considered, leading to more comprehensive and effective change initiatives.

Iterative development is another fundamental approach in agile change management. This involves breaking down the change process into smaller, manageable segments or iterations. Each iteration delivers a part of the overall change, allowing for gradual implementation. This method enables organizations to test and refine changes in real-time, reducing the risk associated with large-scale transformations. It also allows for quicker adaptation as feedback is received and integrated at each stage.

Feedback loops are integral to the agile approach. Continuous feedback from employees, customers, and other stakeholders is actively sought and used to inform the change process. These feedback loops ensure that the change remains relevant and aligned with the needs and expectations of those affected by it. Regularly incorporating feedback also helps in identifying potential issues early, allowing for timely adjustments.

In addition to these approaches, agile change management often involves regular review and reflection sessions. These sessions, sometimes known as retrospectives, provide an opportunity for the team to discuss what is working and what needs improvement. This reflection is crucial for learning and continuous improvement.

Visual management tools, such as Kanban boards or agile project management software, are also commonly used. These tools provide a clear overview of the progress of change initiatives, helping to track tasks, manage workflow, and ensure transparency among team members. Fostering a culture that supports experimentation and learning from failures is important in agile change management. Encouraging a mindset where it is safe to take calculated risks and learn from mistakes is essential for fostering innovation and adaptability.

Addressing and overcoming resistance to change within organizations is a crucial aspect of successful change management. Resistance often stems from fear of the unknown, discomfort with new processes, or a perceived threat to job security. Effective strategies to manage and mitigate this resistance are essential.

One key strategy is effective communication. Clearly and transparently communicating the reasons for the change, the benefits it will bring, and how it will be implemented can alleviate fears and misunderstandings. Communication should be ongoing, not just at the outset of the change process, and should be two-way, allowing for employee feedback and concerns to be heard. Involving employees in the change process can significantly reduce resistance. When employees are part of the decision-making process, or at least have a platform to voice their opinions and contribute ideas, they are more likely to buy into the change. This involvement can be achieved through workshops, focus groups, or regular meetings.

Providing adequate training and support is another crucial strategy. Employees may resist change if they feel they lack the skills or understanding to navigate the new system or process. Offering comprehensive training and ongoing support can help employees feel more confident and competent, reducing resistance.

Leadership plays a critical role in managing resistance to change. Leaders should model the behavior they want to see, demonstrating commitment to the change and a positive attitude towards it. Strong leadership can inspire and motivate employees to embrace change. Recognizing and addressing the emotional impact of change is also important. Change can be unsettling, and acknowledging the emotional side of change can help in managing resistance. This might involve providing counseling services, peer support programs, or simply creating a space where employees can express their feelings and concerns.

Offering incentives can be an effective way to overcome resistance. Incentives can be financial, but they can also be in the form of career advancement opportunities, public recognition, or other non-monetary benefits. Identifying and working with change champions can aid in overcoming resistance. Change champions are individuals who are enthusiastic about the change and can influence their peers positively. They can be instrumental in spreading a positive message about the change and addressing their colleagues' concerns.

Facilitating agile change management effectively involves utilizing specific tools and techniques that enable organizations to respond swiftly and efficiently to change. These tools and techniques are designed to enhance collaboration, streamline processes, and ensure continuous feedback and improvement.

Agile Project Management Software

Tools like Jira, Trello, or Asana are essential for managing change projects in an agile environment. They enable teams to organize tasks, track progress, and adapt plans quickly based on current needs. These platforms often include features like Kanban boards and Scrum boards, which are particularly useful for visualizing workflow and managing iterative progress.

Collaboration Platforms

Tools such as Slack, Microsoft Teams, or Zoom facilitate communication and collaboration among team members, regardless of their location. They are crucial for daily check-ins, impromptu discussions, and maintaining a continuous flow of information, which is vital in agile environments.

Feedback and Survey Tools

Platforms like SurveyMonkey, Qualtrics, or TinyPulse help gather feedback from employees and stakeholders. Regular feedback is key in agile change management to understand the impact of changes and to make timely adjustments.

Document Sharing and Collaboration Tools

Google Drive, Dropbox, or Microsoft SharePoint allow for real-time document sharing and collaboration. These tools are essential for maintaining version control and ensuring that all team members have access to the latest information.

Mind Mapping Software

Tools like MindMeister or XMind are useful for brainstorming sessions and organizing thoughts and ideas visually. They can be particularly helpful in the planning stages of a change initiative.

Digital Whiteboarding Tools

Platforms like Miro or Mural replicate the experience of a physical whiteboard, providing a shared space for remote teams to brainstorm, plan, and visualize ideas and processes.

Change Management Software

Specific change management tools, like Prosci's ADKAR Model or ChangeScout, can help in structuring and guiding the change process, offering methodologies and frameworks tailored to agile change management.

Performance Tracking Tools

Tools like Tableau or Google Analytics can be used to track and analyze performance data. This is important for measuring the impact of changes and making data-driven decisions.

Timeboxing Techniques

Using timeboxing to allocate a fixed time period for tasks or meetings helps in maintaining focus and momentum, which is important in agile environments.

Retrospective Tools

Tools like Retrium or FunRetro facilitate conducting retrospective meetings to review what went well and what could be improved. These sessions are critical for continuous improvement in agile change management.

By incorporating these tools and techniques, organizations can enhance their ability to manage change in an agile and responsive manner, adapting to new challenges and seizing opportunities more effectively.

Aligning Culture with Agile Practices

Aligning agile change management practices with existing organizational culture requires a thoughtful and strategic approach. This alignment ensures that the introduction and implementation of agile practices complement and enhance the current culture, rather than clashing with it.

Understanding the existing culture is the first step. Assess the current organizational values, norms, and behaviors. This understanding helps in identifying aspects of the culture that are conducive to agile practices and those that may need adaptation. It's essential to recognize the strengths of the current culture and leverage them in the transition to agile change management.

Communication is key in this alignment process. Clearly articulating the benefits of agile change management and how it aligns with the organization's goals and values can foster acceptance and support. Communicating the vision and objectives of this shift, and how it will impact the organization positively, is crucial for gaining buy-in. Involving employees at all levels in the transition process is also important. Seek input and feedback from employees and involve them in planning and implementation. This participatory approach not only ensures that the agile practices are tailored to fit the organization but also helps in building commitment and ownership among employees.

Training and education are vital components of aligning agile practices with organizational culture. Providing training on agile methodologies, principles, and tools helps employees understand and embrace these new ways of working. It's important that training goes beyond just the technical aspects and addresses how agile practices fit into the broader organizational context.

Adapting leadership styles to support agile change management is essential. Leaders should model agile behaviors such as flexibility, openness to change, and collaborative decision-making. Leadership development programs can be useful in equipping leaders with the skills and mindsets needed for leading agile transformations. Piloting agile practices in smaller teams or projects before a full-scale roll-out can help in assessing how these practices fit with the existing culture. It allows for adjustments and refinements to be made based on real experience within the organization's unique context.

Recognizing and celebrating early successes of agile change management can help in building momentum and demonstrating its value. Highlighting how these successes align with and enhance the existing culture reinforces the compatibility of agile practices with the organization. It's important to be patient and persistent. Cultural change is a gradual process, and aligning agile change management practices with existing culture takes time. Continuous monitoring, feedback, and adjustments are key to ensuring a smooth and successful integration.

By taking these steps, organizations can effectively align agile change management practices with their existing culture, ensuring a seamless transition that leverages the strengths of the current culture while introducing new, agile ways of working.

Cultivating a culture that embraces continuous improvement and learning is critical for organizations to remain competitive and innovative in today's rapidly changing business environment. This culture fosters adaptability, resilience, and a proactive approach to challenges and opportunities.

Toyota, with its pioneering Toyota Production System, exemplifies the significance of a culture rooted in continuous improvement. Central to their philosophy is the concept of 'Kaizen', which means continuous improvement in Japanese. Toyota encourages all employees, from the factory floor to management, to constantly look for ways to improve processes and reduce waste. This culture of continual incremental improvements has not only made Toyota one of the most efficient and profitable automakers but also a model for manufacturing and business processes worldwide.

Google, known for its innovative practices, places a strong emphasis on learning and experimentation. Google's famous '20% time' – where employees are encouraged to spend 20% of their time working on projects outside of their routine responsibilities – has led to the development of key products like Gmail and AdSense. This culture of experimentation and learning from both success and failure drives Google's capacity for innovation and adaptation.

Microsoft, under the leadership of Satya Nadella, has undergone a cultural transformation with a renewed focus on a 'learn-it-all' culture as opposed to a 'know-it-all' culture. This shift, emphasizing continuous learning and growth mindset, has been instrumental in Microsoft's recent successes and rejuvenation. It has fostered an environment where employees are motivated to learn new skills and adapt to changing technologies, keeping the company at the forefront of the tech industry.

Salesforce is another example where a culture of continuous learning and improvement is deeply embedded. The company's online learning platform, Trailhead, is not just for customers but also for its employees, encouraging them to continuously develop their skills and stay up-to-date with the latest trends and technologies. This culture of ongoing learning and self-improvement has been key to Salesforce's rapid growth and ability to stay ahead in the competitive CRM market.

These examples demonstrate that cultivating a culture of continuous improvement and learning can lead to significant benefits, including increased efficiency, innovation, employee satisfaction, and adaptability to change. It creates organizations that are agile, forward-thinking, and prepared to meet the challenges of the modern business world.

Leadership's Role in Culture and Agile Change Management

The critical role of leadership in shaping and guiding organizational culture cannot be overstated. The saying "the fish rots from the head" aptly underscores the impact that leaders have on the health and direction of an organization's culture. Leadership sets the tone, establishes norms, and models behaviors that permeate throughout the organization.

Leaders are the primary architects and stewards of organizational culture. Their actions, decisions, and communication styles are closely observed and often emulated by employees. When leaders prioritize transparency, ethical behavior, and open communication, these values become ingrained in the organizational culture. Conversely, if leaders exhibit negative behaviors such as secrecy, inconsistency, or lack of integrity, it can foster a toxic culture that undermines trust and engagement.

For example, Satya Nadella's leadership at Microsoft transformed the company's culture from one known for internal competition to a culture of collaboration and innovation. Nadella's emphasis on a "growth mindset" encouraged employees to learn from failures, be open to change, and continuously improve. This cultural shift played a significant role in revitalizing Microsoft's innovation and market position.

Apple's culture of innovation and attention to detail is often attributed to the leadership style of Steve Jobs. His relentless focus on product design and user experience shaped Apple's culture, driving the company to produce groundbreaking products and maintain a dominant position in the technology sector.

Leaders also play a pivotal role in guiding organizations through cultural transformations, particularly during times of change such as mergers, acquisitions, or shifts in strategic direction. Effective leaders understand the importance of aligning the culture with the organization's vision and goals. They actively engage with employees at all levels to ensure that the culture evolves in a way that supports the organization's objectives. Leadership's role in cultural development extends to how they handle challenges and crises. The way leaders respond to difficult situations can significantly impact the organizational culture. For instance, how a leader addresses a mistake or a failure – whether they take responsibility, learn from it, and move forward – sets an example for the rest of the organization.

Leadership is crucial in shaping and guiding organizational culture. Leaders not only set the initial direction for the culture but also nurture and adapt it over time. Their behaviors, values, and attitudes are mirrored throughout the organization, making their role central to developing a positive, healthy, and sustainable organizational culture.

Effectively leading and managing agile change initiatives requires leaders to adopt a set of practices and mindsets that are conducive to agility and responsiveness. Here are key insights into how leaders can successfully steer agile change in their organizations:

Embrace a Visionary Yet Flexible Leadership Style: Leaders should have a clear vision for the change initiative but also remain open to adapting their approach based on feedback and changing circumstances. This balance between a steadfast vision and flexibility is crucial in agile environments.

Foster a Culture of Open Communication and Collaboration: Leaders should encourage open lines of communication and foster a collaborative environment. This involves not just sharing information transparently but also actively listening to feedback from all levels of the organization and incorporating that feedback into the change process.

1. Empower Team Members: Agile change thrives in an environment where team members feel empowered to make decisions and take action. Leaders should delegate authority and provide teams with the autonomy to manage their work, encouraging a sense of ownership and responsibility.

2. Promote Continuous Learning and Adaptability: Leaders should encourage a culture of continuous learning, where team members are open to acquiring new skills and adapting to new methods. This could involve providing access to training resources, encouraging experimentation, and creating an environment where it's safe to take risks and learn from failures.

3. Practice Iterative Development: Break down the change initiative into smaller, manageable segments or iterations. This approach allows for testing and refining changes incrementally, making the process more manageable and less risky.

4. Utilize Agile Tools and Techniques: Implement agile project management tools and techniques such as Scrum or Kanban to manage tasks and workflows. These tools help in maintaining visibility of progress and ensure that the team stays aligned.

5. Lead by Example: Leaders should model agile behaviors themselves. This includes being adaptable, receptive to feedback, and willing to make quick decisions. Leading by example is one of the most powerful ways to instill an agile culture.

6. Focus on Customer and Stakeholder Value: Keep the focus on delivering value to customers and stakeholders. Leaders should ensure that every aspect of the change initiative is aligned with enhancing customer experience or stakeholder value.

7. Build Resilience and Handle Setbacks Positively: Change is often accompanied by challenges and setbacks. Leaders need to build resilience within their teams and handle these setbacks positively, viewing them as opportunities for learning and growth.

8. Celebrate Milestones and Successes: Recognizing and celebrating milestones and successes in the change process can boost morale and reinforce the value of the agile approach.

Several organizations across various industries have successfully implemented agile change management, demonstrating its effectiveness in driving innovation, efficiency, and adaptability. Here are some real-world success stories:

- Spotify's approach to agile change management, particularly in its engineering and product development teams, is a notable success story. The company adopted a unique model known as "Spotify Model," which emphasizes autonomous, cross-functional teams called "squads," each responsible for specific aspects of the product. This structure allows for rapid iteration and responsiveness to changes in the market or customer preferences, contributing significantly to Spotify's ability to innovate and stay ahead in the competitive music streaming industry.

- ING, a Dutch multinational banking corporation, underwent a significant agile transformation. In an effort to better respond to customer needs and digital competition, ING restructured its organization into agile teams, resembling a more tech company-like environment. This shift involved dissolving traditional departments and creating multidisciplinary teams, which improved the speed and efficiency of their service delivery and product development.

- Known for its engineering and technology products, Bosch implemented agile methodologies to improve innovation and adaptability. The company adopted a large-scale agile framework that involved restructuring into smaller, cross-functional teams, enabling faster decision-making and a more responsive approach to product development. This shift not only improved product development cycles but also enhanced employee satisfaction and engagement.

- The defense and aerospace company, SAAB, adopted agile practices to manage complex product development in a highly regulated industry. By implementing agile methodologies, SAAB was able to improve collaboration across various departments, enhance product quality, and reduce time-to-market for new products, all while maintaining strict compliance with industry regulations.

- Barclays, the British multinational bank, embarked on an agile transformation to improve efficiency and customer service. The change involved a cultural shift towards greater collaboration, transparency, and continuous improvement. By adopting agile methodologies, Barclays improved its ability to respond to customer needs and market changes rapidly, leading to enhanced service delivery and operational efficiency.

The case studies of Spotify, ING Bank, Bosch, SAAB, and Barclays offer a wealth of insights into the effective implementation of agile change management, each illustrating key aspects of this approach in action. A central theme across these examples is the cultivation of a company culture that emphasizes flexibility, autonomy, and empowerment. Spotify's squad-based structure and ING's shift to multidisciplinary teams highlight how empowering smaller, cross-functional groups can lead to more efficient and innovative outcomes.

Adaptability to market changes and customer preferences is another critical lesson. Spotify's ability to swiftly adjust its offerings based on user feedback underlines the significance of maintaining a customer-centric focus in agile methodologies. Continuous learning and improvement emerge as essential elements for success. Bosch's experience shows that adopting agile methodologies not only improves product development cycles but also positively impacts employee engagement, demonstrating that continuous improvement benefits both product quality and team morale.

Enhanced collaboration is a key benefit of agile change management. SAAB's approach to breaking down silos and encouraging collaboration across departments leads to better outcomes, particularly in complex project environments. The role of leadership in driving and sustaining agile transformation is also a vital lesson. Barclays' agile journey exemplifies how leadership commitment and a top-down approach to cultural change are crucial for a successful transformation.

Agility can be effectively applied even in highly regulated industries, as shown by SAAB. This case study illustrates that agility and compliance can coexist, provided the right approach is adopted. The need to balance structure with flexibility is a significant takeaway. While agile methodologies promote adaptability and rapid change, maintaining a level of structure and clear goals, as seen in Bosch and ING's transitions, is essential for keeping teams focused and aligned.

These real-world examples provide comprehensive insights into successfully navigating agile change management, emphasizing the importance of a flexible and empowering culture, adaptability to customer needs, continuous learning, cross-functional collaboration, committed leadership, agility in various contexts, and balancing flexibility with structure.

In this chapter, we delved into the nuances of agile change management and its increasing relevance in today's fast-paced business environment. The main themes and strategies discussed centered around how organizations can effectively implement and benefit from agile principles in managing change. We began by defining agile change management, emphasizing its focus on flexibility, responsiveness, and iterative progress. This approach contrasts with traditional change management methods by being more adaptive and responsive to the changing business landscape. The importance of cultivating a culture that embraces continuous improvement and learning was highlighted as a crucial aspect of agile change management. We discussed how this culture fosters adaptability and resilience, enabling organizations to stay competitive and responsive to changes.

Key principles of agile change management, including cross-functional teamwork, iterative development, and regular feedback loops, were explored. These principles ensure that change initiatives are flexible, collaborative, and continually refined based on real-time feedback and learning.

We also discussed various practical tools and techniques for facilitating agile change management. These include agile project management software, collaboration platforms, and feedback tools, all of which help in streamlining the change process and enhancing team coordination. The chapter emphasized the critical role of leadership in shaping and guiding organizational culture towards agility. Leaders not only set the tone for the change but also play a pivotal role in modeling agile behaviors and practices.

Real-world success stories from organizations like Spotify, ING Bank, Bosch, SAAB, and Barclays provided concrete examples of agile change management in action. These case studies illustrated the benefits of agile methodologies in enhancing innovation, efficiency, and adaptability.

Key lessons from these case studies were discussed, offering insights into the benefits of a flexible and empowering culture, the importance of customer-centricity, the need for continuous learning, and the effectiveness of cross-functional collaboration in driving agile change.

The chapter presented a comprehensive overview of agile change management, its principles, practices, and real-world applications. It underscored the importance of adaptability, resilience, and continuous improvement in today's business world and provided practical guidance on how organizations can successfully embrace and benefit from agile change management practices.

As we move forward from our in-depth exploration of agile change management and its integration within organizational culture, we transition seamlessly into the next chapter, which delves into Complex Human Behaviors and New Work Realities. This chapter will build upon the foundations laid in our discussion of agile methodologies and cultural adaptability, exploring how these elements interact with and are influenced by complex human behaviors in contemporary work settings.

In the upcoming chapter, we will examine the multifaceted nature of human behavior within organizations, especially in light of the new realities of work – such as increased remote working, digital collaboration, and evolving workforce dynamics. We will explore how understanding and addressing these complex behaviors is crucial for effectively implementing agile change management and fostering a supportive organizational culture. We will also delve into the psychological aspects of work in the modern era, discussing how factors like motivation, engagement, and job satisfaction are impacted by new work realities. The chapter will consider the implications of these changes on leadership styles, team dynamics, and overall organizational effectiveness. We also investigate the challenges and opportunities that arise from these new work realities. This includes understanding the impact of technology on human behavior, navigating the challenges of remote and hybrid work models, and leveraging the opportunities they present for enhancing collaboration and innovation.

By linking the concepts of agile change management and organizational culture with the study of complex human behaviors and new work realities, the next chapter aims to provide a holistic understanding of the contemporary workplace. This understanding is essential for leaders and organizations seeking to thrive in an ever-evolving business landscape.

4. Complex Human Behaviors and New Work Realities

The purpose of this chapter is to explore the intricate behavioral shifts and the emergence of new organizational structures in the post-COVID era. It delves into how the pandemic has not just altered the physical aspects of work but also led to profound changes in employee behaviors, management practices, and the very fabric of organizational dynamics. A key focus is on understanding how employee engagement and motivation have evolved in the wake of widespread remote work. The chapter examines the strategies organizations have employed to keep a geographically dispersed workforce engaged and the innovative approaches that have emerged to motivate employees outside the traditional office environment.

Another critical aspect is the management of employee well-being, with a special emphasis on mental health and burnout in a remote or hybrid work setting. This includes an analysis of how organizations are navigating the challenges of maintaining work-life balance for their employees and the steps taken to address burnout more effectively and compassionately.

The chapter also explores the evolution of organizational structures. With the shift to remote and hybrid models, traditional hierarchical models are giving way to more flexible, agile, and responsive structures. This section investigates how these new structures are influencing organizational culture, decision-making processes, and overall business agility.

Leadership in the post-COVID world is another significant area of focus. The chapter analyzes how leadership styles have adapted to manage continuous change and uncertainty, emphasizing the increasing importance of empathy, resilience, and flexible decision-making in leaders.

Performance management in the new work environment is also a critical topic. The chapter discusses the challenges and opportunities in redefining performance metrics and evaluations to suit remote and hybrid work settings. The chapter addresses the complexities of ensuring diversity, equity, and inclusion in a remote work environment. It highlights the innovative practices organizations are implementing to create an inclusive workplace that transcends physical boundaries.

The COVID-19 pandemic has not only brought fundamental changes to the work and organizational behavior but also presented more nuanced challenges in the post-pandemic era. A significant issue has been redefining employee engagement and motivation in a predominantly remote work environment. This shift demanded innovative approaches to keep a physically distant workforce motivated and engaged. Alongside this, managing burnout became a critical concern, particularly in remote settings where the traditional office boundaries blurred, making it difficult to recognize and address burnout effectively.

Another complex aspect has been navigating the hybrid work paradox. Organizations moving towards hybrid models grappled with the challenge of managing two distinct work environments: the physical office and remote work. Ensuring fairness and productivity in these varied settings added layers of complexity to workforce management. This situation also led to challenges in maintaining cultural cohesion within a distributed workforce. The absence of physical interactions, which traditionally supported organizational culture, required new strategies to sustain company values and culture across diverse locations.

With the shift to remote operations, heightened cybersecurity risks emerged as a significant concern. Organizations had to fortify their digital communication and data protection strategies to address the increased vulnerability to cybersecurity threats. Concurrently, adapting to rapid technological changes became essential, requiring continuous learning and adaptation from both the organization and its employees.

Addressing mental health stigma and providing adequate support in the workplace also became a nuanced challenge. Creating an environment conducive to discussing and seeking help for mental health issues was paramount for employee well-being. Leadership styles too underwent a transformation. The continuous change and uncertainty demanded a shift from traditional leadership approaches to ones characterized by empathy, flexibility, and resilience.

Reimagining performance management for a remote or hybrid work setting was another intricate task. Traditional performance evaluation metrics often proved inadequate, necessitating the development of new frameworks that accurately reflect performance in these new work environments. Finally, ensuring diversity, equity, and inclusion in remote settings required intentional and innovative efforts. Organizations had to find ways to create inclusive practices that transcended the physical boundaries of traditional office spaces. See below a Table that describes each of these new challenges for leadership.

Redefining Employee Engagement and Motivation: With remote work becoming more prevalent, traditional approaches to employee engagement faced challenges. Organizations had to find new ways to motivate and engage a workforce that was no longer physically present in a centralized location.

Managing Burnout in a Remote Setting: The blurring lines between work and personal life led to increased instances of burnout. Identifying and addressing burnout in a remote setting, where physical cues are absent, became a critical challenge for organizations.

Navigating the Hybrid Work Paradox: As some organizations moved towards hybrid models, they faced the paradox of managing two distinct work environments: in-office and remote. Ensuring fairness, engagement, and productivity across these different settings posed a complex challenge.

Cultural Cohesion in a Distributed Workforce: Maintaining a cohesive organizational culture when employees are distributed across various locations became a nuanced challenge. Organizations had to rethink how to instill and sustain their values and culture without the physical interactions that traditionally supported them.

Heightened Cybersecurity Risks: The shift to remote work increased the organization's exposure to cybersecurity threats. Ensuring secure digital communication and protecting sensitive data in a dispersed work environment required new strategies and tools.

Adapting to Rapid Technological Changes: The accelerated adoption of new technologies necessitated continuous learning and adaptation. Organizations had to support their employees in upskilling and reskilling to keep pace with these changes.

Mental Health Stigma and Support: While there was an increased focus on mental health, a nuanced challenge was addressing the stigma around it and providing adequate support. Creating an environment where employees felt comfortable seeking help was crucial.

Leadership in Times of Continuous Change: Leaders had to navigate not just the immediate crisis but also the ongoing uncertainty and change. This required a shift from traditional command-and-control leadership to more empathetic, flexible, and resilient leadership styles.

Reimagining Performance Management: Traditional performance metrics and evaluations were often unsuitable for the new work environment. Organizations needed to develop new frameworks that accurately reflected performance in a remote or hybrid setting.

Diversity, Equity, and Inclusion in Remote Settings: Ensuring diversity, equity, and inclusion became more complex in a remote work environment. Organizations had to be intentional in their efforts to create inclusive practices that transcended physical boundaries.

Behavioral Shifts Pre- and Post-COVID

Before the COVID-19 pandemic, organizational behavior across various industries was characterized by a set of widely accepted practices that shaped the corporate culture and daily operations. Central to these practices was the concept of a centralized work environment, where employees typically worked from a designated office space. This physical proximity not only facilitated direct supervision but also fostered face-to-face interactions, contributing to a sense of community and collaboration among team members.

Organizations predominantly operated under traditional hierarchical structures, with clear lines of authority and decision-making processes. This often led to a top-down approach in management and communication. Alongside this, the concept of standardized working hours, usually encapsulated in the typical 9-to-5 workday, provided a uniform framework for managing workloads and coordinating team efforts.

In-person communication and collaboration were pivotal in organizational communications. Meetings, brainstorming sessions, and collaborative projects were predominantly conducted in person, utilizing meeting rooms and communal spaces. When it came to performance evaluations, these were generally formal and structured, conducted at regular intervals and focusing primarily on individual achievements and goal completion.

Organizations also relied heavily on standardized policies and procedures to guide employee behavior and organizational processes. These policies were often uniform across the organization, offering little flexibility or personalization. The physical office space held significant importance, seen as a symbol of corporate culture, status, and brand identity, with its design and layout considered crucial to fostering a productive work environment.

Remote work, while present, was not the norm and was often reserved for specific roles or circumstances, with the majority of employees expected to be physically present in the office. Leadership styles were more conventional, focusing on control, consistency, and adherence to established processes and standards. Finally, there was a general emphasis on maintaining stability and predictability in business operations, with a focus on long-term planning and risk aversion.

The COVID-19 pandemic has reshaped organizational behavior in profound ways, prompting a deeper and more nuanced transformation in the workplace. These changes extend beyond the initial adaptations and have fundamentally altered how organizations operate, engage employees, and manage challenges.

In redefining employee engagement and motivation, the focus has shifted from traditional in-person interactions to creating a virtual environment that fosters a sense of community and purpose. This involves not just digitalizing existing processes but also innovating new ways to connect and engage with employees. For instance, virtual social gatherings and digital recognition platforms have become vital in keeping the workforce engaged and motivated. Additionally, personalized engagement strategies tailored to individual employee needs have gained prominence, recognizing that remote work affects each employee differently.

Addressing burnout in a remote setting has become a critical focus area. Organizations are now actively developing strategies to create a sustainable work-life balance for remote employees. This includes implementing flexible work policies, encouraging regular digital detoxes, and creating an organizational culture that prioritizes mental health. The role of managers has also evolved, with an increased emphasis on being attuned to the well-being of their teams and providing support for mental health challenges.

Navigating the hybrid work paradox involves balancing the needs and experiences of both remote and in-office employees. This includes redesigning work processes to be location-agnostic, ensuring that remote employees have equal access to opportunities and resources as their in-office counterparts. There is a growing emphasis on creating a level playing field for all employees, regardless of their physical location, which involves rethinking career development paths and performance evaluation criteria to accommodate the hybrid model.

Maintaining cultural cohesion in a distributed workforce has become more complex. Organizations are finding creative ways to transmit their culture and values across digital platforms. This might involve virtual team-building activities that are culturally relevant or using internal communication platforms to share stories and experiences that reinforce the organization's values. The challenge is to create a sense of shared purpose and identity that resonates with employees in diverse locations. The heightened cybersecurity risks associated with remote work have led organizations to invest significantly in their IT infrastructure. This goes beyond implementing advanced security measures; it involves cultivating a culture of cybersecurity awareness among employees. Regular training sessions, simulations of phishing attacks, and clear guidelines on data security have become part of the organizational routine.

Adapting to rapid technological changes has also been a critical area of focus. Organizations are not only adopting new technologies but are also ensuring that their workforce is equipped to leverage these technologies effectively. This requires continuous skill development and training programs, along with fostering a culture of innovation where employees are encouraged to explore and adopt new digital tools.

The adaptation to the changes brought by the COVID-19 pandemic has been a journey of learning and resilience for both employees and leaders. This adaptation has manifested in various ways, including shifts in work habits, communication styles, and stress management techniques.

Shifts in Work Habits

Employees have had to redefine their work routines and habits to suit remote or hybrid working environments. This has often meant creating dedicated workspaces at home, establishing new routines to start and end the workday, and adopting self-discipline to manage distractions. Time management has become a critical skill, with employees learning to balance work tasks with personal responsibilities, especially in remote settings where the lines between work and personal life can blur.

Adaptation in Communication Styles

Communication styles have undergone a significant shift. In the absence of face-to-face interactions, both employees and leaders have had to become proficient in digital communication tools. This includes not just mastering the technology but also learning the nuances of virtual communication, such as maintaining engagement during video calls and effectively conveying messages through written communication. There's also an increased emphasis on over-communication to ensure clarity and prevent misunderstandings in the absence of physical cues.

Embracing Digital Collaboration

Collaboration has taken on a new dimension with the use of digital tools. Employees have adapted to collaborating on projects through digital platforms, learning to navigate and leverage various software for teamwork. This change has fostered an environment where digital proficiency is crucial, and continuous learning and adaptation to new tools are a norm.

Enhanced Focus on Stress Management

The pandemic has heightened awareness around mental health and stress management. Employees and leaders alike have had to find new ways to manage stress in uncertain times. This includes adopting mindfulness practices, engaging in regular physical exercise, and seeking support through employee assistance programs or mental health resources. There's been a noticeable shift towards acknowledging and openly discussing mental health in the workplace.

Leadership Adaptations

Leaders have had to adapt their styles to suit remote and hybrid teams. This has involved becoming more empathetic and understanding of the challenges faced by their teams. Many leaders have shifted towards a more inclusive and consultative leadership style, prioritizing communication and employee well-being. They've also had to become adept at managing teams virtually, which includes fostering team cohesion, maintaining morale, and ensuring productivity in a remote setting.

Innovative Problem-Solving and Decision Making

The unpredictability brought about by the pandemic has required both employees and leaders to become more agile in their problem-solving and decision-making. There's been a shift towards more innovative, creative solutions to tackle the unique challenges presented by the new working conditions.

The COVID-19 pandemic has introduced various changes in the workplace, some of which are likely to be temporary, while others may become entrenched in the post-pandemic world.

Temporary changes include the extreme reliance on virtual meetings. While virtual communication will remain a key aspect of business operations, the intensity and frequency of these meetings are expected to reduce as organizations strike a balance with in-person interactions. Additionally, the high levels of remote work witnessed during the pandemic may not sustain indefinitely. Many organizations are likely to adopt a hybrid work model rather than a fully remote one. The rapid technological adoption that marked the pandemic period was driven by urgent necessity. Post-pandemic, this pace might slow as organizations align technology adoption with long-term strategic goals.

On the other hand, several changes are poised to become permanent. The shift towards flexible work arrangements has demonstrated significant benefits in productivity and employee satisfaction, indicating that this flexibility will likely be a lasting aspect of work culture. The increased focus on employee well-being, particularly regarding mental health and work-life balance, emerged as a critical consideration during the pandemic and is expected to continue as a mainstay in organizational priorities.

The use of digital collaboration tools has transformed teamwork and communication. These tools, having proven their effectiveness, are expected to remain integral in work environments, supplementing traditional in-person collaboration. The pandemic also necessitated a shift towards more decentralized decision-making, empowering mid-level managers and teams for quicker, more responsive action. This approach is likely to continue, given its benefits in increasing organizational agility and responsiveness.

The emphasis on agility and resilience, vital during the pandemic's uncertain times, is expected to inform future organizational strategies and cultures. The focus on creating diverse and inclusive work environments has also been accelerated by the pandemic. This trend, driven by social movements and the recognized benefits of a diverse workforce, is likely to endure, reflecting a broader evolution in workplace culture that values flexibility, inclusivity, and digital proficiency.

Emerging Organizational Structures

The rise of decentralized organizational structures, especially accelerated by the COVID-19 pandemic, marks a pivotal shift in business operations, moving away from traditional hierarchical models. These structures are characterized by their approach to distributing decision-making authority, empowering lower-level employees, and fostering flexibility and responsiveness. In decentralized organizations, decision-making is spread throughout various levels, allowing for quicker, more localized responses to changes and challenges. This empowerment of lower-level employees can lead to increased motivation and job satisfaction due to a greater sense of ownership in their work.

One of the key advantages of decentralized models is their ability to make decisions quickly. Without the need for decisions to travel up and down a hierarchical chain, responses to market changes or customer needs can be more immediate. This structure also enhances employee engagement, as individuals feel a direct impact from their contributions. Additionally, the spread of decision-making authority helps in reducing bottlenecks that typically occur in centralized systems.

Decentralized models come with their own set of challenges. One significant risk is the potential for inconsistency in decisions across different parts of the organization, which may not always align with the overall strategic direction. Effective communication becomes vital to ensure that all parts of the organization are aligned and working towards common goals. Managing a decentralized organization can be complex, requiring a balance between giving autonomy to various units and maintaining a degree of centralized control to ensure coherence and unity. Additionally, allocating resources efficiently across different decentralized units can be a challenge, as each unit might have varying needs and priorities.

Network-based organizational models have gained prominence, especially in the rapidly evolving business landscape shaped by technological advances and globalization. These models stand out for their flexibility, adaptability, and capacity to foster innovation, making them particularly suited to the demands of the modern business environment.

At the core of a network-based organization is the principle of flexibility. Unlike traditional hierarchical structures, network-based models are characterized by a web of connections where nodes (individuals or teams) can interact and collaborate in various configurations. This flexibility allows for quick realignment and reconfiguration in response to changing business needs or market conditions, enabling a more dynamic approach to project management and problem-solving.

Adaptability is another key feature of network-based organizations. These models thrive on their ability to adapt rapidly to external changes. By leveraging a decentralized structure, decisions can be made swiftly and close to the source of action, which is particularly advantageous in fast-paced or unpredictable markets. This adaptability extends to the workforce as well, with employees often taking on multiple roles or moving between projects as needed, contributing to a more agile and responsive organization.

Network-based models are particularly conducive to innovation. The open structure encourages a free flow of information and ideas among different parts of the organization, fostering creative problem-solving and innovation. Employees are often encouraged to collaborate across traditional boundaries, bringing diverse perspectives and expertise to the table. This cross-pollination of ideas is a key driver of innovation, as it allows for unconventional approaches and solutions to emerge. These models often leverage technology to support their networked structure, utilizing digital collaboration tools to connect team members across different locations and time zones. This technological aspect not only supports the operational functioning of the network but also contributes to a culture of continuous learning and adaptation, which is essential for innovation.

Network-based organizations also tend to have a more organic approach to growth and development. Rather than following a predetermined path, these organizations evolve naturally based on the interactions and collaborations within the network. This organic growth can lead to unexpected opportunities and innovations, as the organization is not constrained by a rigid structure or plan.

The emergence of hybrid work environments, blending remote and in-office work, has significantly impacted organizational structures, signaling a shift from traditional office-centric models to more flexible arrangements. This hybrid model, accelerated by the COVID-19 pandemic, has introduced both opportunities and challenges for organizations as they adapt to this new way of working.

Hybrid work environments offer flexibility, allowing employees to split their time between working from home and the office. This flexibility has shown to improve work-life balance and employee satisfaction, leading to potential increases in productivity and engagement. For employers, this flexibility can lead to a reduction in overhead costs associated with maintaining full-time office spaces. These models also necessitate changes in organizational structures. One of the key impacts is the need for more dynamic and adaptable management practices. Leaders and managers must learn to effectively supervise and engage teams that are not always physically present, requiring a shift in communication strategies and performance evaluation methods. Trust and accountability become even more crucial in these environments.

The technology infrastructure of organizations has also had to evolve to support hybrid work. This includes investing in secure and efficient communication and collaboration tools that facilitate seamless working regardless of location. Organizations have had to ensure that both remote and in-office setups are equipped with the necessary technology to maintain productivity and connectivity.

Another impact is on organizational culture. Maintaining a cohesive culture in a hybrid environment can be challenging, as traditional methods of team building, and employee engagement might not be as effective. Organizations are finding new ways to foster a sense of community and shared purpose among employees who may not physically meet regularly. The hybrid model also influences office space utilization and design. With not all employees in the office at the same time, organizations are rethinking their physical spaces, often moving towards more collaborative and flexible layouts rather than fixed individual workstations. These types of work environments have implications for diversity and inclusion. They can offer more equitable opportunities for those who may have been marginalized by traditional office setups, such as people with disabilities or caregiving responsibilities. However, there is also the risk of creating a divide between remote and in-office employees, potentially leading to disparities in access to resources, opportunities, and networking.

Navigating New Organizational Realities

The evolving organizational structures, especially with the rise of decentralized, network-based models, and hybrid work environments, necessitate a significant adaptation in leadership styles and strategies. Leaders are finding that the traditional command-and-control approach is less effective in these dynamic settings and are therefore adopting more flexible, inclusive, and empathetic leadership styles. Flexibility in leadership has become crucial. Leaders must be able to adapt their approach based on the situation, the team's needs, and the specific dynamics of the work environment. This might mean shifting between hands-on guidance for remote teams and a more autonomous approach for in-office teams or adapting communication styles to suit different mediums and settings.

Inclusivity in leadership is also more important than ever. Leaders need to ensure that all team members, whether working remotely or in the office, feel included and valued. This involves being mindful of the unique challenges faced by remote workers, such as potential feelings of isolation or being out of the loop on informal communications that happen in the office. Effective leaders actively work to create opportunities for all team members to contribute and be heard.

Empathy has emerged as a key trait in effective leadership. Understanding and acknowledging the diverse personal and professional challenges that team members face, particularly in the context of the pandemic, is critical. Leaders who show empathy can build trust and foster a supportive team environment, which is vital for maintaining morale and productivity in these challenging times.

Communication strategies have also had to evolve. Leaders need to be clear, consistent, and transparent in their communication, ensuring that all team members, regardless of their location, have access to the same information and feel equally informed. This might involve leveraging various technology platforms to facilitate communication and making an extra effort to reach out to remote team members.

Leaders are adopting a more collaborative approach to decision-making. Encouraging input and feedback from team members can lead to more innovative solutions and helps in building a sense of shared ownership and responsibility. This collaborative approach is particularly effective in decentralized and network-based structures, where diverse perspectives can greatly enhance problem-solving and innovation.

The focus on continuous learning and development is another key aspect of leadership in these emerging structures. Leaders need to not only keep themselves updated with the latest trends and technologies but also encourage and facilitate continuous learning for their teams. This approach is crucial for staying agile and adaptable in a rapidly changing business environment. Maintaining organizational culture and cohesion in decentralized and network-based models requires innovative strategies that address the unique challenges of these structures. With decision-making and operations spread across various nodes in the network, ensuring a unified culture and a sense of cohesion becomes vital for the overall effectiveness and identity of the organization.

One key strategy is to emphasize and consistently communicate the organization's core values and mission. In decentralized and network-based models, where employees may have varying degrees of autonomy and might not interact frequently with central leadership, it's crucial that everyone understands and aligns with the fundamental principles and goals of the organization. Regular communication of these values, through digital channels, meetings, and company-wide events, helps in reinforcing the organizational identity.

Creating opportunities for connection and interaction across different parts of the organization is also essential. This can be achieved through cross-functional projects, inter-departmental meetings, or virtual social events. Such interactions not only facilitate knowledge sharing and collaboration but also help in building a sense of community among employees who may not physically work together.

Leaders play a critical role in maintaining culture and cohesion. They should act as role models, embodying and reflecting the organization's values in their actions and decisions. Effective leaders in decentralized settings also focus on building trust and empowerment within their teams, fostering a culture where employees feel valued and motivated. Leveraging technology is another important aspect. Digital platforms that facilitate communication, collaboration, and social interaction can help maintain a sense of connectedness among employees. These platforms can range from project management tools to virtual meeting spaces and social channels, all aimed at creating a virtual environment that supports the organization's cultural dynamics.

Recognition and celebration of successes and milestones contribute significantly to a cohesive culture. Acknowledging individual and team achievements, even in a distributed setting, can boost morale and reinforce a sense of belonging. Celebrations can be conducted virtually, ensuring everyone, regardless of their location, can participate and feel included.

Encouraging and facilitating feedback loops is crucial in decentralized models. Regular surveys, open forums, and feedback channels allow employees to voice their opinions and contribute to the organization's continuous improvement. This not only helps in addressing any issues that might arise but also makes employees feel heard and valued. Training and development initiatives that focus on the organization's culture can be beneficial. These initiatives can include leadership development programs that emphasize cultural leadership or onboarding processes that introduce new employees to the organization's values and ways of working.

The Role of Technology in Shaping Behaviors

Technology has played a pivotal role in shaping new work behaviors and organizational structures, especially in the context of recent global shifts. Its influence can be seen in various aspects of how organizations operate and how employees engage with their work. It has enabled the widespread adoption of remote and hybrid work models. Tools like video conferencing, cloud computing, and collaborative software have made it possible for teams to work effectively from different locations. This technological enablement has not only changed where employees work but also how they work, leading to more flexible work schedules and a greater emphasis on work output rather than hours spent in the office.

The rise of digital communication platforms has altered traditional communication patterns within organizations. With less reliance on face-to-face interactions, there's been a shift towards asynchronous communication, where team members collaborate and communicate across different time zones and schedules. This shift has also necessitated new norms and etiquettes for digital communication, emphasizing clarity, conciseness, and responsiveness.

Technology has also facilitated flatter and network-based organizational structures. With enhanced communication and collaboration tools, decision-making and information-sharing processes can be more decentralized, allowing for quicker responses and greater empowerment of individual employees or teams. This decentralization can lead to more innovative and agile organizations, as ideas and feedback can flow more freely across the organization without being bottlenecked by hierarchy.

Data analytics and artificial intelligence (AI) have introduced new ways of working and decision-making. Organizations can now leverage data-driven insights to make more informed decisions, predict trends, and personalize customer and employee experiences. AI and automation are also reshaping job roles and responsibilities, automating routine tasks, and allowing employees to focus on more strategic and creative work.

The evolution of technology has also brought challenges, particularly in terms of cybersecurity and the digital divide. As reliance on digital platforms increases, so does the vulnerability to cyber threats, making robust cybersecurity measures essential. Additionally, ensuring all employees have access to and are proficient with necessary technologies is crucial for equitable participation in the new work environment.

In terms of organizational culture, technology has had a significant impact. Building and maintaining a cohesive culture in a technologically driven, often dispersed work environment requires deliberate efforts. Organizations are using digital tools not just for work-related tasks but also for virtual team-building, social interactions, and cultural initiatives, ensuring a sense of community and shared values. Effectively leveraging technology in new work realities involves harnessing digital tools to enhance communication, collaboration, and productivity. In a landscape where remote and hybrid work models are prevalent, technology plays a central role in ensuring that teams can work efficiently and cohesively.

For communication, it's crucial to utilize a mix of synchronous and asynchronous tools. Synchronous tools like video conferencing platforms (e.g., Zoom, Microsoft Teams) are essential for real-time meetings and discussions, helping maintain a sense of immediacy and connection. Asynchronous tools like email, messaging apps (e.g., Slack, Microsoft Teams), and project management software (e.g., Asana, Trello) allow for flexible communication that respects individual schedules and time zones. The key is to establish clear guidelines on how and when to use these tools to avoid miscommunication and digital overload.

Collaboration is significantly enhanced through cloud-based platforms and shared digital workspaces. Tools like Google Workspace or Microsoft 365 enable teams to work on documents, spreadsheets, and presentations simultaneously, regardless of their physical location. These platforms facilitate a seamless flow of ideas and real-time feedback, which is essential for maintaining momentum on projects and tasks.

To boost productivity, organizations can leverage task management software that helps in tracking progress, setting deadlines, and assigning responsibilities. This clarity and organization can prevent tasks from falling through the cracks, especially in a decentralized working environment. Time-tracking tools and productivity apps can also help individuals manage their time more effectively, especially in a remote setting where self-discipline is key. Another aspect of leveraging technology is using data analytics tools to gain insights into work patterns, team performance, and project progress. These insights can inform decision-making, help identify areas for improvement, and ensure resources are allocated efficiently.

Technology also plays a role in creating an inclusive and engaging work environment. Digital tools for employee engagement, like virtual team-building activities, online training sessions, and digital "water coolers" for informal interactions, can help maintain a sense of community and belonging among team members. It's also important to provide training and support for these technologies. Ensuring that all employees are comfortable and proficient with the tools they need to use is essential for effective communication, collaboration, and productivity. Regular training sessions, user guides, and IT support can aid in this process.

Cybersecurity measures are another critical aspect of leveraging technology. As work becomes more digitized, protecting sensitive information and maintaining robust cybersecurity protocols is paramount. Regular updates, secure access controls, and employee training on cybersecurity best practices are necessary to safeguard organizational data.

There are noteworthy examples of organizations that have successfully adapted to behavioral shifts and adopted new organizational structures in response to the evolving work landscape:

Twitter's Early Adoption of Remote Work

Twitter was one of the first major tech companies to announce that its employees could continue working from home indefinitely, even after the pandemic subsides. This decision was a significant shift from the traditional tech work culture and highlighted the company's flexibility and adaptability in response to employee needs and global trends.

Unilever's Focus on Employee Well-being and Flexible Work

Consumer goods giant Unilever has been a frontrunner in promoting flexible working arrangements and focusing on employee well-being. They implemented a global remote working policy and invested in digital tools to support collaboration and productivity. Unilever also launched initiatives for mental health support and work-life balance, demonstrating a commitment to adapting their organizational culture to new realities.

Salesforce's "Success from Anywhere" Model

Salesforce introduced its "Success from Anywhere" model, allowing employees more freedom to choose how, when, and where they work. This model is a blend of in-office and remote work, aiming to provide flexibility while maintaining a sense of community and collaboration. Salesforce also redesigned its office spaces to serve as community hubs to support customer and employee engagement in this new hybrid environment.

Accenture's Fluid Workforce and Digital Acceleration

Consulting giant Accenture has embraced a fluid workforce model, leveraging their global presence to enable employees to work in dynamic, cross-geographical teams. Alongside this, Accenture has accelerated its digital transformation, investing in cloud technologies and AI to facilitate efficient remote work and client services.

Novartis' Emphasis on High Performance with Flexibility

Pharmaceutical company Novartis implemented a new "choice with responsibility" work model, which emphasizes high performance combined with flexible working arrangements. The company empowers its employees to choose how they work most effectively, recognizing that this flexibility can lead to higher productivity and job satisfaction.

The case studies of organizations like Twitter, Unilever, Salesforce, Accenture, and Novartis adapting to new work realities provide a wealth of insights into the evolving landscape of work. One of the most significant trends observed is the shift towards embracing flexibility and autonomy in work arrangements. This approach, which allows employees to choose where and how they work, acknowledges the diverse needs and preferences within the workforce and is linked to higher levels of job satisfaction and productivity.

These companies also show a strong commitment to investing in digital infrastructure. The emphasis on digital transformation, evident in the adoption of cloud technologies and collaboration platforms, is essential for supporting remote and hybrid work models. This focus on digital tools is not just a response to immediate needs but a long-term strategic investment, indicating a sustained commitment to flexible work arrangements.

Employee well-being has emerged as a key focus area. Initiatives for mental health, work-life balance, and well-being programs are increasingly integral to these new work models, recognizing the crucial role of employee health and happiness in productivity and retention.

Another key learning is the redefinition of organizational culture. As work models shift, there's a need to adapt organizational cultures to support these new environments. Efforts to maintain a sense of community and collaboration, even in a distributed setting, are central to these efforts. A notable shift from monitoring hours worked to focusing on outcomes and productivity marks a change in how work is evaluated and managed. This results-oriented approach respects individual working styles and is conducive to efficiency and creativity.

Effective leadership in these evolving environments is characterized by adaptability, empathy, and support. Leaders are crucial in driving the adoption of new practices and ensuring that teams remain cohesive and aligned with organizational goals, irrespective of where the work is being done. These organizations are also catering to a wider range of employee needs, promoting inclusivity and diversity by offering various working models. Such flexibility makes the workplace more accessible and accommodating for different groups, including those with caregiving responsibilities or disabilities. An emphasis on continuous learning and innovation is evident. Keeping pace with new technologies and work practices requires a commitment to learning and adapting, which is essential for staying competitive in a rapidly changing business environment. These examples reflect a broader transformation in workplace practices, highlighting the importance of flexibility, digital enablement, employee well-being, a results-focused work culture, adaptive leadership, inclusivity, and a commitment to continuous learning and innovation.

This chapter has delved into the significant transformations in organizational behavior and structures in the face of rapidly changing work environments, highlighting several key insights and strategies. The shift towards remote and hybrid work models is a central theme, reflecting a broader move towards workplace flexibility. This shift necessitates new approaches to work, including redefining employee engagement and motivation in a landscape where traditional in-person interactions are less frequent.

A major insight is the importance of maintaining organizational culture and cohesion in decentralized and network-based structures. Strategies to achieve this include consistent communication of core values, leveraging technology for collaboration, and creating opportunities for interaction across different parts of the organization.

The chapter also underscores the need for adaptability in leadership styles. Modern leaders are required to be more empathetic, inclusive, and supportive, acknowledging the diverse needs of their teams, especially in remote or hybrid settings. Technology's role in these transformations is highlighted, with a focus on how digital tools can enhance communication, collaboration, and productivity. Investing in digital infrastructure and fostering a culture of continuous learning and innovation are identified as key strategies for success.

Addressing the challenges of managing change and transitions in these new organizational forms is another important focus. Effective change management involves clear communication, involving employees in the change process, providing adequate training and support, and being flexible and responsive to feedback. Real-world examples of organizations that have successfully navigated these changes provide practical insights. These case studies demonstrate the effectiveness of embracing flexibility, focusing on employee well-being, investing in digital capabilities, and maintaining a strong organizational culture in the face of significant change.

We now transition from exploring the transformative shifts in organizational structures and work behaviors, to an equally crucial and interconnected topic: the interplay of these new realities with diversity, equity, and flexible work modes. The next chapter delves into how the evolving work landscape, shaped by digital transformation and shifting organizational norms, intersects with and influences diversity and equity within the workplace.

We will explore how remote and hybrid work models, by their very nature, open up new avenues for inclusivity, offering opportunities for a more diverse range of individuals to participate in the workforce. These models can break down traditional barriers, offering greater accessibility to individuals who may have been marginalized by conventional office-based work structures.

The chapter will also examine the challenges and responsibilities that come with these changes. As organizations navigate these new work modes, ensuring equitable access to opportunities and resources for all employees, regardless of their work location or schedule, becomes imperative. We will discuss strategies for fostering an inclusive work environment that supports diversity and promotes equity, considering factors like unconscious bias, communication barriers, and cultural differences.

We'll dive into how flexible work modes can be leveraged to support a diverse workforce, examining policies and practices that accommodate varying needs and life circumstances. From flexible scheduling to tailored benefits and support systems, we will look at how organizations can create a work environment that not only embraces diversity but also actively supports the well-being and success of all its members.

5. Leadership in Diverse and Flexible Work Modes

Today's organizations are characterized by a diversity of work modes, each presenting its own set of dynamics and challenges. These modes – in-person, hybrid, and fully remote – have become increasingly prevalent and are reshaping the landscape of workplace interaction and leadership.

In-Person Work Mode

Traditional in-person work environments, where team members work together in a physical office space, have long been the standard. This mode fosters direct face-to-face interaction, spontaneous communication, and can strengthen team cohesiveness. However, it also requires leaders to navigate the challenges of managing on-site dynamics, including workspace collaboration and conflict resolution.

Hybrid Work Mode

The hybrid model has emerged as a blend of in-person and remote work, offering greater flexibility. In this mode, some employees work on-site, while others work remotely, either on a set schedule or as determined by individual or team needs. This mode demands leaders to balance and integrate the needs and experiences of both remote and in-person team members, ensuring equity and inclusivity in team interactions and opportunities.

Fully Remote Work Mode

Fully remote work, where all team members operate outside of a traditional office environment, gained significant traction due to the COVID-19 pandemic. This mode eliminates geographical constraints, allowing for a broader talent pool, but also challenges leaders to maintain team cohesion, communication, and culture in a virtual environment.

In this chapter, we will explore how leaders can effectively navigate and lead within these diverse work modes. We will delve into the unique challenges and opportunities each mode presents and offer strategies for effective leadership tailored to the nuances of in-person, hybrid, and fully remote teams. The goal is to equip leaders with the insights and tools needed to adapt their leadership styles to a changing work landscape, ensuring effectiveness, inclusivity, and productivity in whichever mode their organization operates.

Leadership in In-Person Settings

Traditional in-person leadership dynamics, while seemingly challenged by the rise of remote and hybrid work models, still hold significant relevance in the modern workplace. In-person settings offer unique dynamics that can greatly influence leadership effectiveness and team performance. In a traditional in-person environment, leadership relies heavily on face-to-face interactions. These interactions facilitate immediate feedback, clearer communication, and stronger relationship-building. The physical presence of leaders can have a profound impact on team morale and engagement. Leaders can more easily gauge team members' reactions and emotions, allowing for more effective and empathetic management.

Another aspect of in-person leadership is the ability to foster a cohesive team culture. Physical office spaces often create a sense of community and belonging, which can be leveraged by leaders to build team spirit and collaboration. The shared physical environment also provides opportunities for spontaneous interactions and informal communication, which are invaluable for creative brainstorming and problem-solving.

Traditional leadership in an office setting often involves more direct oversight of team activities. Leaders can observe work processes, provide immediate guidance, and quickly intervene when issues arise. This can lead to more efficient decision-making and problem resolution. The relevance of these traditional dynamics in the modern workplace must be balanced with the evolving expectations of employees. Today's workforce often values flexibility, autonomy, and work-life balance, which can sometimes be at odds with the more structured nature of in-person work environments.

Effective leaders in a modern in-person setting are those who can blend traditional leadership strengths — such as direct communication and hands-on guidance — with an appreciation for more contemporary values like employee autonomy, wellness, and professional development. This balanced approach ensures that the benefits of in-person interactions are harnessed effectively while adapting to the changing landscape of employee needs and expectations.

In-person leadership has undergone significant evolution to meet the challenges of today's work environment, characterized by rapid technological advancement and shifting employee expectations. Modern in-person leaders are adapting their approaches in several keyways:

1. Integrating Technology: Today's in-person work environments are heavily infused with technology. Leaders are incorporating digital tools for various purposes, including project management, real-time collaboration, and effective communication. The use of technology enhances efficiency and productivity in the workplace. Leaders must be adept at choosing and implementing the right technologies that complement and enhance the traditional office setting.

2. Embracing Flexibility and Autonomy: Modern employees often seek greater flexibility and autonomy in their roles. In response, leaders are adopting a more flexible approach to work arrangements, even in in-person settings. This might include flexible hours, opportunities for telecommuting, or a results-oriented work environment (ROWE) where the focus

is on outcomes rather than the number of hours spent in the office.

3. Fostering a Culture of Continuous Learning: The rapid pace of change in today's business world requires a workforce that is skilled, adaptable, and continuously evolving. Leaders are creating environments where continuous learning and development are part of the organizational culture. This includes providing opportunities for professional growth, upskilling, and reskilling, as well as encouraging a mindset of lifelong learning.

4. Prioritizing Employee Well-being: Modern leaders recognize the importance of employee well-being and its impact on productivity and satisfaction. This has led to an increased focus on initiatives that promote work-life balance, mental health, and overall wellness. Leaders are implementing policies and practices that support employee well-being, such as wellness programs, mental health days, and ergonomic workspaces.

5. Building a Diverse and Inclusive Culture: Modern leaders understand the value of diversity and inclusion in driving innovation and business success. Efforts are being made to create an inclusive culture where diverse perspectives are valued, and employees feel a sense of belonging. This includes diversity and inclusion training, fair and unbiased recruitment practices, and support for employee resource groups.

6. Encouraging Collaboration and Teamwork: Despite the rise of individual autonomy, collaboration and teamwork remain essential. Leaders are finding new ways to foster collaboration in the workplace, such as designing collaborative workspaces, using team-building activities, and encouraging cross-departmental projects.

7. Enhancing Communication: Effective communication is more critical than ever. Leaders are refining their communication skills to be more transparent, empathetic, and inclusive. They

are also leveraging digital tools to enhance communication and ensure that important messages are conveyed clearly and effectively.

In adapting to these modern challenges, in-person leadership is becoming more dynamic, employee-centric, and technology-driven. Leaders who successfully navigate these changes can create a work environment that is productive, engaging, and aligned with the needs and expectations of the modern workforce.

Leadership in Hybrid Work Environments

Hybrid work models, where teams are partially remote and partially in-person, present a unique set of challenges and opportunities for leaders and organizations.

Challenges of Hybrid Work Models

- Maintaining Fairness and Inclusivity: One of the main challenges is ensuring that remote employees don't feel left out or less important than their in-person counterparts. There's a risk of creating a two-tier system where in-office employees have more visibility and access to information than remote workers.

- Communication Barriers: Effective communication can be more complex in a hybrid setup. Ensuring that all team members, regardless of their location, receive the same level of information and can contribute equally to discussions requires deliberate communication strategies.

- Collaboration Dynamics: Fostering collaboration between remote and in-person team members can be challenging. Leaders must find ways to facilitate seamless collaboration and teamwork, ensuring that no team member is isolated or disadvantaged by their work location.

- Performance Evaluation: Assessing performance in a hybrid model can be tricky, especially if evaluations are biased towards more visible in-office behaviors. Leaders need to develop fair and equitable performance metrics that accurately reflect the contributions of both remote and in-person employees.

- Building Team Culture: Creating a cohesive team culture in a hybrid environment requires extra effort. Leaders need to find ways to instill shared values and a sense of belonging among team members who may have different experiences and interactions with the organization.

Opportunities in Hybrid Work Models

- Increased Flexibility and Autonomy: Hybrid models offer employees greater flexibility and autonomy in choosing their work environment, which can lead to increased job satisfaction and productivity.

- Broader Talent Pool: Hybrid models allow organizations to tap into a wider talent pool, not limited by geographical constraints. This can lead to more diverse teams with a broader range of skills and perspectives.

- Improved Work-Life Balance: For many employees, hybrid models provide a better balance between professional and personal life, leading to improved well-being and reduced burnout.

- Innovation in Work Practices: The hybrid model encourages innovation in work practices, pushing organizations to find new and efficient ways of working, communicating, and collaborating.

- Cost-Effective Operations: Organizations can benefit from reduced office space and associated costs, as not all employees are in the office at the same time.

To successfully navigate the hybrid work model, leaders must be proactive in addressing its challenges while capitalizing on its opportunities. This involves creating inclusive communication and collaboration strategies, implementing fair performance metrics, and fostering a strong and cohesive team culture that bridges the gap between remote and in-person work environments.

In hybrid work settings, leaders face the unique challenge of bridging the divide between remote and in-office employees. To navigate this successfully, a strategic approach that emphasizes clear communication, inclusivity, and a balance of needs is essential. The cornerstone of effective leadership in a hybrid environment is clear and consistent communication. Leaders must establish regular communication routines, ensuring that both remote and in-office team members are equally informed and connected. This could involve a mix of weekly team meetings, daily check-ins, and regular email updates. The goal is to create a communication framework where every team member, regardless of location, feels informed and included.

Utilizing technology effectively is another key aspect. Digital tools like video conferencing, instant messaging, and collaborative project management software can significantly reduce the physical distance between remote and in-office team members. These tools facilitate not just formal meetings and project collaboration, but also spontaneous interactions and casual conversations. Inclusivity during meetings is particularly crucial. Leaders should ensure that remote participants are given equal opportunities to contribute, with technology enabling them to engage effectively. This might mean prioritizing screen sharing for presentations or using virtual whiteboards for brainstorming sessions.

A culture of flexibility can greatly enhance the hybrid work experience. Recognizing the different challenges faced by remote and in-office employees, and accommodating these variations in work styles, can help meet diverse needs. Whether it's flexibility in work hours, deadlines, or communication preferences, such an approach acknowledges and respects individual working conditions. Setting clear guidelines and expectations is vital for managing the diverse dynamics of hybrid teams. Leaders should clearly articulate work hours, availability, communication norms, and performance metrics for both remote and in-office employees. This clarity helps manage expectations and reduces potential misunderstandings.

Promoting team cohesion involves creating opportunities for team bonding that cater to both remote and in-office employees. Leaders might organize virtual team-building activities, online social events, or in-person gatherings where remote employees are also present, ensuring everyone feels part of the team. Encouraging open feedback allows leaders to understand the effectiveness of their hybrid work strategies. Creating channels where employees can express their views on the hybrid model and being open to making adjustments based on this feedback, ensures continuous improvement.

Supporting and normalizing remote work is also crucial. Leaders should treat remote work as an integral part of the organizational culture, providing necessary support in terms of technology and resources. Recognizing and addressing the unique challenges faced by both remote and in-office employees is essential. This includes being attentive to feelings of isolation among remote workers and managing the potential for overwork among in-office employees. Balancing informal interactions is key. Leaders should encourage informal virtual interactions to mimic in-office dynamics, ensuring remote employees are not excluded from casual networking and relationship-building.

Leading in a hybrid environment is about creating a cohesive, inclusive, and adaptable work culture. It requires a nuanced approach where communication, technology, flexibility, and empathy are woven together to meet the diverse needs of all team members.

Leadership in Fully Remote Teams

Leading teams that operate entirely remotely involves navigating a unique set of challenges and opportunities. The lack of physical interaction necessitates a distinct approach to leadership, focusing on building trust, maintaining engagement, and ensuring productivity. Building trust in a remote team is foundational and starts with transparency. Leaders need to communicate openly and regularly, sharing both successes and challenges of the business. This openness fosters a culture of trust and encourages team members to be equally transparent. Trust is also built by showing reliability and consistency in actions and decisions, and by giving team members autonomy, demonstrating confidence in their abilities.

Maintaining engagement in a remote setting requires proactive efforts. Regular virtual check-ins and team meetings are essential, not just for work-related discussions but also for social interaction and team bonding. Creating opportunities for informal engagement, such as virtual coffee breaks or social hours, can help replicate the office environment's camaraderie. Recognizing and celebrating achievements, providing constructive feedback, and showing appreciation for hard work are also crucial for keeping team members motivated and engaged.

Ensuring productivity in a remote team is often about setting clear expectations and providing the right tools and resources. This includes defining clear goals and deliverables and equipping the team with effective communication and collaboration tools. It's important to focus on outcomes rather than the number of hours worked, which aligns with the remote work ethos of flexibility and autonomy. Leaders must also be attentive to the work-life balance of their team members. Remote work can blur the boundaries between personal and professional life, so leaders should encourage their teams to take regular breaks and respect non-working hours. This approach not only prevents burnout but also contributes to sustained productivity and well-being.

Another aspect of leading remote teams is fostering a sense of belonging and connection to the organization. This involves not only ensuring that team members understand the company's vision and goals but also feel that they are an integral part of achieving them. Leaders should facilitate regular communication about the company's direction and how each team member's work contributes to the broader picture. Adapting to the nuances of remote leadership also means being more mindful of individual differences. This includes understanding and accommodating different working styles, time zones, and personal circumstances. Tailoring communication and management approaches to suit individual team members can significantly enhance team cohesion and effectiveness.

Best practices for remote leadership have become increasingly important as more organizations embrace remote work. Effective remote leadership involves a blend of strategic use of digital tools, clear communication, and fostering a strong remote work culture.

Utilizing Digital Tools

In a remote work setting, digital tools are the lifeline of communication and collaboration. Leaders must be adept at selecting and utilizing the right tools for different needs. This includes video conferencing tools like Zoom or Microsoft Teams for face-to-face interaction, collaboration platforms like Slack for continuous communication, and project management tools such as Asana or Trello for tracking tasks and progress. The effective use of these tools helps in maintaining connectivity, collaboration, and workflow management in a remote setting.

Clear and Consistent Communication

Clear communication becomes even more crucial in a remote environment. Leaders should establish regular communication schedules, such as daily check-ins and weekly team meetings, to ensure consistent touchpoints. It's important to communicate expectations clearly, especially regarding work hours, availability, project deadlines, and performance metrics. Moreover, communication should not just be task-oriented; it should also include check-ins on employees' well-being.

Fostering a Strong Remote Work Culture

Creating a sense of community and shared culture in a remote team is vital. This involves building a culture that supports flexibility, encourages collaboration, and values work-life balance. Leaders should encourage an environment where team members feel comfortable sharing their ideas and challenges. Regular virtual team-building activities and informal interactions can help strengthen relationships and build a sense of belonging.

Empowering and Trusting Team Members

Empowerment is key in remote settings. Leaders should trust their team members to manage their tasks and provide them with the autonomy to make decisions regarding their work. This empowerment boosts morale and drives engagement.

Encouraging Professional Development

Continuous learning should be a part of the remote work culture. Leaders can encourage professional growth by providing access to online learning resources, webinars, and virtual workshops. This not only aids in skill development but also keeps the team members engaged and motivated.

Personalized Leadership Approach

Recognizing that each team member may have different needs and preferences in a remote work setting is important. Personalizing communication and management approach based on individual team members' styles can significantly enhance effectiveness.

Feedback and Recognition

Regular feedback is essential for remote teams. Constructive feedback helps team members understand how they can improve, while recognition of their efforts and achievements boosts morale and reinforces positive behaviors.

Addressing Challenges Proactively

Remote work comes with its set of challenges, such as feelings of isolation or burnout. Leaders should be proactive in addressing these challenges, offering support, resources, and solutions where needed.

Effective remote leadership requires a combination of leveraging digital tools effectively, communicating clearly and consistently, fostering a strong remote work culture, empowering team members, supporting their development, personalizing leadership approaches, providing feedback and recognition, and proactively addressing the unique challenges of remote work. These practices ensure that the remote team not only remains productive but also feels connected and valued.

Leading Through Uncertainty

Leading through uncertainty, especially in the context of shifting work modes, presents a complex challenge for leaders. These uncertainties arise from rapidly changing organizational needs and evolving global circumstances, which can significantly impact the way businesses operate and teams collaborate.

One of the major uncertainties stems from the evolving nature of work itself. The transition to remote or hybrid models, accelerated by the COVID-19 pandemic, has reshaped the traditional office environment. This shift has introduced questions about the long-term viability and structure of these work models, as organizations grapple with what the future of work looks like for them. Decisions around maintaining fully remote teams, returning to in-person work, or adopting a hybrid model are fraught with uncertainties regarding productivity, employee well-being, and collaboration.

Changing organizational needs add another layer of complexity. As businesses navigate through uncertain economic conditions, technological advancements, and competitive landscapes, their strategies and goals can shift rapidly. This may require quick pivots in operations, realignment of teams, and reevaluation of business models. Leaders must navigate these changes while maintaining team focus and morale.

Global circumstances, such as economic volatility, political unrest, and public health crises, further contribute to the uncertainty. These factors can have far-reaching effects on business operations, from disrupting supply chains to shifting consumer behavior. Leaders must be prepared to respond to these external factors, often with limited information and time to decide. Leading through this uncertainty requires a set of adaptable and resilient leadership skills. Leaders must be able to make informed decisions quickly, often in situations where there is no precedent. They need to communicate with clarity and confidence, even when the path forward is not entirely clear, to provide direction and reassurance to their teams.

Leaders must foster a culture that is flexible and responsive to change. Encouraging innovation, supporting risk-taking, and promoting a mindset of continuous learning can help teams adapt to evolving circumstances. Being transparent about the challenges and involving team members in finding solutions can also help in navigating uncertainties more effectively. Emotional intelligence is another crucial component of leading through uncertainty. Understanding and addressing the concerns and anxieties of team members, and providing support where needed, is essential for maintaining team cohesion and morale in challenging times.

Navigating the uncertainties of shifting work modes in the modern workplace requires leaders to employ nuanced and specific strategies. A key approach is developing scenario-based planning, where leaders analyze potential future scenarios and formulate strategic responses to each. This helps organizations prepare for a range of possible outcomes.

Creating an environment of psychological safety is also crucial. Leaders need to cultivate a space where team members feel comfortable expressing ideas and concerns, which is essential for fostering open dialogue and innovation. This involves showing empathy and actively seeking input from all team members, especially those who might be less vocal. Enhancing the team's digital dexterity goes beyond providing the right tools; it involves training team members to use these tools effectively and encouraging exploration of new technologies. This enhances the team's ability to adapt to various digital work environments.

As remote work often leads to global team compositions, cultivating cultural intelligence becomes essential. Leaders need to be aware of and respect different cultural backgrounds and work styles, adapting their communication and management practices accordingly. Personalized employee engagement is another important strategy. Recognizing that each team member may be affected differently by uncertainties, leaders should engage with them on a personal level to understand their individual challenges and preferences, tailoring support to meet these needs.

Agile HR practices can also be pivotal in times of uncertainty. Implementing flexible HR policies that cater to diverse employee needs, such as varied working hours and mental health support, can help maintain a motivated and engaged workforce. Utilizing predictive analytics to forecast potential challenges and employee needs can provide leaders with valuable insights, allowing them to anticipate and mitigate issues such as burnout or disengagement.

Building a resilience toolkit for teams, including resources on stress management, mindfulness, and adaptability, can equip team members with the skills to navigate through challenging times. Workshops or training sessions on building personal resilience can be particularly beneficial. Adopting dynamic goal setting is also essential. In an uncertain environment, static goals may quickly become outdated, necessitating regular review and adjustment of objectives in response to changing circumstances.

Encouraging cross-functional collaboration is crucial for combating silos that might develop in remote or hybrid settings. This not only fosters innovation but also enhances understanding and cooperation across different parts of the organization. By implementing these nuanced approaches, leaders can effectively guide their teams through the complexities and uncertainties of today's evolving work landscape, ensuring adaptability, cohesion, and continued growth.

Balancing Consistency and Flexibility in Leadership

Maintaining consistent leadership principles and practices across different work settings is crucial for several reasons. In a world where work environments can vary widely – from traditional in-office settings to fully remote or hybrid models – consistency in leadership ensures a stable and coherent experience for all team members, regardless of their physical location or working conditions. Consistency in leadership fosters trust and reliability within the team. When team members know what to expect from their leaders, regardless of the work setting, it builds a sense of security and predictability. This trust is particularly important in remote or hybrid environments, where physical distance can sometimes lead to feelings of disconnect or uncertainty.

Consistent leadership practices help in establishing and reinforcing the organization's culture. A strong organizational culture, underpinned by consistent values and behaviors from the leadership, provides a guiding framework for employees. It shapes how they interact, make decisions, and approach their work, leading to a more cohesive and aligned workforce. This kind of leadership is also key to ensuring fairness and equity. In hybrid environments, for instance, there's a potential risk of creating disparities between remote and in-office employees. Consistent leadership practices ensure that all team members, irrespective of their work setting, are treated equally, have access to the same opportunities, and are evaluated by the same standards.

Maintaining consistency in leadership across various work settings contributes to clearer communication. When leaders are consistent in how they communicate – be it the frequency, medium, or messaging – it reduces the likelihood of confusion and misunderstandings, enhancing overall team efficiency and collaboration. It's important to note that consistency does not imply rigidity. Effective leaders are also adaptable, able to modify their approaches to fit the unique demands of different work settings while still upholding core principles and practices. For instance, the way feedback is delivered might need to be adapted for remote settings, but the commitment to providing regular, constructive feedback remains constant.

This kind of adapting leadership approach to meet the specific needs of a team's work mode is a critical skill in today's diverse work environments. While maintaining consistent principles, leaders also need to be flexible and responsive to the unique challenges and opportunities presented by different work modes.

In traditional in-person settings, leaders can take advantage of face-to-face interactions to build strong relationships, observe team dynamics firsthand, and provide immediate feedback. They can also foster team cohesion through in-person meetings, team-building activities, and informal interactions. However, they must be mindful of providing sufficient autonomy and not micromanaging, given the physical proximity to team members.

For remote teams, leaders need to rely more on technology to communicate and collaborate. This involves not just selecting the right digital tools but also being adept at using them to maintain team connectivity and workflow. Regular virtual check-ins and video conferencing can help mitigate the lack of physical presence. Leaders should also focus on building trust and accountability in a remote setting, where direct oversight is limited. Encouraging open communication and being available for support is key to ensuring remote team members feel connected and valued.

In hybrid work environments, where some team members are remote while others are in-office, leaders face the challenge of balancing these two dynamics. It's essential to ensure inclusivity, making certain that remote employees are not disadvantaged in terms of communication, access to resources, or career opportunities. Leaders might need to implement new practices, such as rotating meeting times to accommodate different time zones or using technology to ensure everyone can participate equally in meetings, regardless of their physical location.

Adapting leadership approaches also means being sensitive to the individual needs of team members. This could involve offering flexible working hours, understanding personal challenges, and providing tailored support to each team member. Leaders should be proactive in seeking feedback on their leadership approach and be willing to make adjustments based on this feedback.

Navigating diverse and flexible work modes requires leaders who can adapt to the changing landscape while maintaining core leadership principles. Here are some case studies showcasing leaders who have successfully managed this balance.

Anne Wojcicki, CEO of 23andMe

Anne Wojcicki, at the helm of the personal genomics company 23andMe, has navigated the shift to remote work by focusing on clear communication and employee well-being. She has been successful in maintaining a strong company culture by prioritizing transparency and supporting her team's needs, which has been especially crucial during the rapid changes brought about by the COVID-19 pandemic.

Stewart Butterfield, CEO of Slack Technologies

As the CEO of a company that provides a platform for remote collaboration, Stewart Butterfield has firsthand experience in managing flexible work modes. He successfully led his team through the pandemic, emphasizing the importance of asynchronous communication and the effective use of digital tools to maintain productivity and team cohesion in a remote environment.

Mary Barra, CEO of General Motors

Mary Barra has been at the forefront of transforming General Motors' work culture, especially in response to the challenges posed by the pandemic. She has effectively balanced in-person and remote work needs, ensuring business continuity while prioritizing employee safety and well-being. Her leadership during this time has been a testament to her ability to adapt to flexible work modes while steering one of the largest automakers in the world.

Eric Yuan, CEO of Zoom Video Communications

Eric Yuan's leadership of Zoom, particularly during a time when the platform became essential for remote work globally, demonstrates his ability to navigate diverse work modes. Yuan has focused on rapidly scaling the company's services while maintaining a strong emphasis on reliability and user experience, a critical aspect of leading a team that enables flexible work for millions.

Arvind Krishna, CEO of IBM

Arvind Krishna has been instrumental in steering IBM through a significant transition to more flexible work modes. Under his leadership, IBM has adopted a hybrid work model, recognizing the benefits of both remote and in-person work. Krishna's focus on digital transformation and employee empowerment showcases his ability to lead a legacy technology company through a period of significant change.

The leadership experiences presented paint a vivid picture of the evolving landscape of modern leadership, particularly in managing diverse and flexible work modes. These leaders exemplify adaptability in their leadership style, recognizing the importance of employee-centric approaches and the strategic use of digital tools. They skillfully navigate external pressures and internal dynamics, all the while fostering a culture of continuous learning and development within their organizations.

In this chapter, we explored the complexities of leadership across diverse work settings, explaining how leaders can effectively navigate the challenges and opportunities presented by traditional in-person, remote, and hybrid work environments. We began by examining traditional in-person leadership dynamics, acknowledging their continued relevance in today's workplace while also noting the need for adaptation to contemporary challenges such as technology integration and evolving employee expectations. The importance of direct interaction, fostering team cohesion, and leveraging physical workspace for spontaneous collaboration and communication were highlighted.

The chapter then shifted to the intricacies of leading in remote and hybrid work settings. We discussed the importance of maintaining consistent leadership principles across these varying environments, emphasizing the need for adaptability in leadership approaches to meet the specific needs of each team's work mode. In remote settings, the focus was on the strategic use of digital tools for communication and collaboration, the importance of clear and regular communication, and the challenges of building trust and maintaining engagement from a distance. The necessity of fostering a strong remote work culture, where flexibility, autonomy, and work-life balance are prioritized, was also discussed.

For hybrid work environments, the chapter explored the unique challenges of managing teams that are partly remote and partly in-person. Strategies for ensuring inclusivity, balancing the needs of remote and in-office employees, and maintaining fairness and equity in communication and opportunities were covered. Real-world examples of leaders provided valuable insights into successfully navigating these diverse work modes. Their experiences underscored the importance of adaptability, clear communication, employee-centric approaches, and the strategic use of technology.

The chapter concluded with an emphasis on the need for flexibility in leadership, alongside the maintenance of consistent core principles. This balance is key to effective leadership in the modern, diverse workplace. By adapting to the specific requirements of each work setting while maintaining a steady vision and approach, leaders can ensure their teams remain cohesive, motivated, and productive, regardless of the work environment.

The next chapter will delve into the multifaceted realm of DEI, examining how leaders can foster an environment where diversity is celebrated, equity is pursued, and inclusion is embedded in the organizational fabric. We will explore how the principles of clear communication, adaptability, and employee-centric approaches, which are essential in diverse work settings, are equally vital in promoting and sustaining DEI within organizations.

The upcoming chapter will also address the challenges and opportunities that leaders face in creating a diverse and inclusive workplace. We will discuss strategies for recognizing and valuing differences, ensuring fair treatment and equal opportunities for all team members, and creating a culture where every employee feels included and empowered to contribute their best.

6. Diversity, Equity, and Inclusion in Leadership

In the upcoming chapter, our focus will shift to the transformative impact of Diversity, Equity, and Inclusion (DEI) principles on leadership practices and team dynamics. The chapter aims to dissect and understand how integrating DEI into the core of organizational leadership can reshape the way teams operate and leaders function. We will explore how DEI principles are no longer just an add-on or a compliance requirement but are increasingly recognized as essential drivers of innovation, employee engagement, and business success. The chapter will delve into how leaders can effectively incorporate these principles into their everyday practices, decision-making processes, and strategic planning.

A key aspect of the chapter will be to examine the ways in which DEI initiatives, when genuinely embraced, can lead to more dynamic, creative, and collaborative team environments. We will look at how diverse perspectives and inclusive practices contribute to richer problem-solving and decision-making processes, and how equity in the workplace leads to more motivated and committed employees. The chapter will also address the challenges leaders face in implementing effective DEI strategies, including overcoming unconscious biases, breaking down systemic barriers, and fostering an inclusive culture that goes beyond surface-level diversity.

We will explore case studies and real-world examples of organizations and leaders who have successfully integrated DEI into their leadership and operational models. These examples will provide valuable insights into practical strategies and the tangible benefits of a strong DEI focus. The aim is to provide a comprehensive understanding of how DEI principles are reshaping leadership and team dynamics in the modern workplace, and how leaders can leverage these principles to build stronger, more effective, and more inclusive organizations.

The nuances of Diversity, Equity, and Inclusion (DEI) in modern leadership mark a significant shift in organizational priorities and societal values, reflecting an evolving landscape of workforce expectations and global interconnectedness. The focus on DEI is more pertinent now than ever due to several factors. Globalization and demographic shifts have created workplaces that are incredibly diverse, necessitating leadership that values and leverages this diversity. Social movements like Black Lives Matter and #MeToo have heightened societal awareness of issues related to equity and inclusion, influencing corporate policies and leadership approaches. Moreover, there's a growing recognition of the link between diverse, inclusive teams and improved business performance and innovation. The ability to attract and retain top talent increasingly hinges on a company's commitment to DEI, as more people seek workplaces that not only represent diversity but actively foster inclusion and equity.

What distinguishes current DEI efforts is a move beyond superficial measures towards genuine inclusivity. This shift is characterized by a focus on creating environments where all employees feel valued and can fully contribute. Addressing unconscious biases, ensuring equitable opportunities, and valuing diverse perspectives are at the heart of these efforts. Organizations are increasingly relying on data analytics to shape their DEI strategies, using metrics to inform and measure the impact of their initiatives.

A key aspect of modern DEI is the acknowledgment of intersectionality, recognizing how overlapping identities affect experiences in the workplace. This approach provides a more comprehensive understanding of diversity and the specific challenges faced by individuals with intersecting marginalized identities.

There's an enhanced focus on holistic wellbeing, including mental health and work-life balance, acknowledging these as critical elements of an inclusive workplace. Leadership development has evolved to include training on managing diverse teams, cultural competency, and bias mitigation, equipping leaders with the necessary skills to foster an inclusive environment.

The Importance of Diversity in Teams

Diversity in the workplace is a multifaceted concept that encompasses a wide range of characteristics and attributes among employees. It goes beyond the traditional notions of race and gender to include various dimensions such as culture, age, thought, sexual orientation, physical abilities, religious beliefs, and socioeconomic backgrounds.

In the context of a team, diversity means having a group of individuals who bring a variety of experiences, perspectives, and skills to the table. Cultural diversity refers to the presence of individuals from various ethnic and cultural backgrounds, enabling a rich exchange of cultural viewpoints and practices. Gender diversity ensures representation across different genders, leading to more balanced and inclusive team dynamics.

Age diversity in teams includes a mix of different generations – from Baby Boomers to Generation Z – each bringing unique viewpoints shaped by their generational experiences. This diversity can lead to a broader range of ideas and a deeper understanding of various market segments. Thought diversity, or cognitive diversity, is the inclusion of people who think differently from each other. This type of diversity is crucial as it encourages innovative problem-solving and decision-making by integrating diverse cognitive approaches, problem-solving strategies, and creative ideas.

The inclusion of diversity in teams brings a multitude of benefits, significantly enhancing their overall performance, creativity, and problem-solving capabilities.

Increased Creativity and Innovation

Diverse teams are fertile grounds for creativity. The amalgamation of different perspectives, experiences, and backgrounds leads to a rich tapestry of ideas. This diversity sparks creativity as team members are exposed to a variety of viewpoints and solutions that they may not have considered otherwise. For instance, a team comprising members from different cultural backgrounds can bring unique insights that contribute to the development of innovative products or services tailored to a global market.

Enhanced Problem-Solving Abilities

Diversity in teams leads to more effective problem-solving. When team members approach problems from various angles, it increases the likelihood of finding robust solutions. Research has shown that diverse groups often outperform more homogenous groups in problem-solving tasks because they process information more carefully and are more innovative in their thinking.

Broader Range of Perspectives

Diverse teams offer a broader range of perspectives, which is invaluable in understanding and responding to the needs of a diverse customer base. For example, a team with a diverse age range can provide insights into different consumer preferences across generations, enabling the company to tailor its products and marketing strategies more effectively.

Improved Decision Making

Diversity in teams leads to more thorough and well-considered decision-making processes. With a variety of viewpoints and a wealth of experiences to draw from, these teams are less prone to groupthink – the tendency to conform to the majority view. This diversity ensures that decisions are not only more inclusive but also more likely to consider the potential impacts on a wider range of stakeholders.

Greater Market Insight

Teams with diverse members can better understand and penetrate diverse markets. Having team members who can relate to different customer segments or geographic markets can provide valuable insights into consumer behavior, cultural nuances, and market trends, leading to more effective marketing strategies and product development.

Enhanced Team Performance and Engagement

Diverse teams often report higher levels of engagement and job satisfaction. When employees feel valued for their unique perspectives and experiences, it fosters a sense of belonging and commitment to the team and the organization. This inclusive environment can lead to higher employee retention rates and better overall team performance.

Managing diverse teams, while beneficial, presents unique challenges that require innovative leadership approaches. The diversity in backgrounds, perspectives, and experiences can lead to complexities in team dynamics that need to be carefully navigated.

Communication Barriers

One of the primary challenges in a diverse team is overcoming communication barriers. This doesn't just refer to language differences, but also to varied communication styles influenced by cultural backgrounds. Leaders must find effective ways to facilitate clear and inclusive communication to ensure that all team members can contribute meaningfully.

Cultural Misunderstandings

Cultural diversity can lead to misunderstandings if cultural norms and practices are not well understood or respected. Leaders must be culturally sensitive and aware, facilitating an understanding among team members to foster a respectful and inclusive environment.

Unconscious Bias and Stereotyping

Unconscious biases and stereotypes can impede the effectiveness of diverse teams. Leaders must be vigilant in identifying and addressing these biases, both in themselves and within the team, to ensure that decisions and interactions are fair and equitable.

Integration and Inclusion

Ensuring that all team members feel included and valued can be challenging, particularly when there are significant differences in backgrounds and experiences. Leaders must actively work to create an inclusive atmosphere where diversity is not just present but is genuinely valued and leveraged.

Conflict Resolution

Diverse teams may have different viewpoints and approaches to work, which can lead to conflicts. Leaders need to be adept at conflict resolution, balancing different perspectives and finding common ground that respects and incorporates diverse viewpoints.

Aligning Diverse Goals and Expectations

Aligning the goals and expectations of a diverse team can be challenging. Leaders must ensure that the team is united in its objectives while also accommodating the diverse motivations and career aspirations of individual team members.

Innovative leadership in this context involves developing and implementing strategies that address these challenges effectively. This might include providing cultural competency training, implementing structured communication channels, fostering a culture of open dialogue and feedback, and actively promoting diversity and inclusion initiatives. Leaders must also model inclusive behavior and encourage team members to appreciate and learn from each other's diverse experiences.

Equity in the Workplace

Equity in an organizational context is a critical concept that extends beyond the premise of equality. It's about understanding and acknowledging the unique circumstances and requirements of each individual and providing the necessary resources and opportunities to ensure equal outcomes for all. In an organization, equity encompasses several key areas. It starts with fair treatment, ensuring that all employees, regardless of their background or identity, are treated with respect and dignity. This involves implementing and upholding policies that prevent discrimination and bias, thus fostering a work environment that is inclusive and respectful.

Access is another crucial aspect of equity in the workplace. It's about ensuring that all employees have access to the tools, resources, and support needed to effectively perform their jobs. Whether it's technology, information, or support systems, equitable access ensures that every employee can succeed in their role. Opportunity in the workplace is also central to the concept of equity. It means providing all employees with equal chances to engage in meaningful projects, partake in training programs, and pursue professional development. Equity in opportunity ensures that every employee has the chance to showcase their abilities and contribute to the organization's success.

When it comes to advancement, equity is about creating transparent and fair processes for career progression. This includes promotions, salary increments, and other forms of professional growth, ensuring they are based on merit and performance rather than favoritism or any form of discrimination. Implementing equity in an organization demands a profound understanding of the different challenges and barriers faced by diverse groups. Leaders must actively work to identify and dismantle systemic inequalities and biases within the organizational structure. This could mean reevaluating recruitment practices, introducing mentorship programs, offering flexible work arrangements, or conducting training to mitigate biases.

Creating and maintaining equitable structures, practices, and policies within an organization is a complex task that requires leaders to be both proactive and dedicated. It begins with a thorough assessment of the organization's existing structures. Leaders need to critically evaluate how these structures may inadvertently perpetuate biases or barriers and then take steps to revise them. This could involve changes in hiring practices, promotion criteria, or work allocation to ensure fairness and equity.

An essential part of promoting equity is the development and implementation of inclusive policies. These policies should cover areas such as non-discrimination, equal opportunity, and accommodation for disabilities, and should be regularly reviewed to keep them up-to-date with the latest understandings of what equity entails.

Training and awareness are pivotal in fostering an equitable workplace. Regular programs that educate employees about unconscious bias, cultural competency, and inclusive communication can play a significant role in building a more equitable organization. Such programs help in raising awareness and guiding employees on how they can contribute to an equitable environment.

A diverse leadership team can significantly impact the promotion of equity. Leaders should strive for diversity at all levels, especially in leadership roles, as diverse leaders are more likely to understand and cater to the needs of a diverse workforce. Encouraging open dialogue is another crucial aspect. Leaders should establish channels through which employees can comfortably share their experiences and provide feedback on equity issues. Regular surveys, feedback sessions, or forums can facilitate this dialogue. Leaders must actively listen to this feedback and be prepared to implement changes based on it.

Measuring the effectiveness of equity initiatives is also important. Leaders should establish metrics to track progress in areas such as diversity in hiring and pay equity, and regularly report on these metrics to maintain transparency and accountability. Accountability mechanisms are key to ensuring that equity is not just a concept but a practice. This involves incorporating equity-related goals into performance evaluations and rewarding those who actively promote an inclusive and equitable work environment.

The role of leaders themselves cannot be understated. They must lead by example, demonstrating their commitment to equity in their actions, decisions, and interactions. When leaders visibly prioritize equity, it reinforces its importance throughout the organization. Through these concerted efforts, leaders can build and sustain an organizational culture that is not only equitable but also inclusive and respectful, thereby enhancing the organization's ability to attract diverse talent, foster innovation, and improve overall performance.

Measuring and assessing equity in organizational practices is essential for ensuring that the principles of fairness and inclusion are not only espoused but also effectively implemented. Organizations can approach this through several methods.

1. Conducting regular audits of hiring, promotion, and compensation practices helps in identifying any disparities that may exist. This involves analyzing data to see if there are patterns of inequality based on gender, race, age, or other demographic factors. Pay equity audits are particularly important to ensure that employees doing similar work are compensated equally, regardless of their background.

2. Employee surveys can be a valuable tool in assessing perceptions of equity within the organization. These surveys should ask direct questions about employees' experiences and perceptions regarding fairness, inclusion, and representation. Analyzing this feedback can provide insights into areas where the organization is succeeding and where improvements are needed.

3. Assessing the diversity of the workforce, especially at the leadership and managerial levels, can be indicative of an organization's commitment to equity. A diverse workforce in terms of race, gender, age, and other factors is often a sign of equitable hiring and promotion practices.

4. Evaluating retention and turnover rates, particularly among underrepresented groups, can also provide insights into equity in the workplace. High turnover rates in these groups might indicate issues with inclusion or career advancement opportunities.

5. Monitoring the participation and outcomes of professional development and leadership training programs can help assess equity in career advancement opportunities. Ensuring that all employees have equal access to these programs and tracking their progress post-training can indicate how equitably these opportunities are being provided.

6. Reviewing employee grievances and complaints related to discrimination or unfair treatment can offer direct insights into where the organization may be falling short in its equity efforts. A high number of such complaints can be a red flag, indicating areas that require immediate attention.

It's important for organizations to not only collect this data but also act on it. The findings should be used to inform policy changes, training programs, and other initiatives aimed at promoting equity. Regularly revisiting these assessment methods ensures that the organization remains on track with its equity goals and adapts to changing dynamics and needs.

Principles of Inclusive Leadership

Inclusive leadership is an approach that emphasizes the value and involvement of every team member in an organization's processes and decision-making. This style of leadership is increasingly important in today's diverse workplace environments, ensuring that a variety of perspectives are not just heard, but actively valued and utilized.

An inclusive leader is characterized by a deep sense of empathy and awareness, enabling them to understand and appreciate the unique experiences and viewpoints of each team member. This understanding is key to creating an environment where everyone feels valued and understood. Such leaders are known for their openness and accessibility. They foster an atmosphere where open communication is encouraged, and team members can share their thoughts and concerns freely, without fear of judgment. This openness is crucial for building trust and ensuring that all voices are heard.

A hallmark of inclusive leadership is fairness and objectivity in decision-making. Inclusive leaders strive to be unbiased, making decisions based on merit and ensuring fairness in all their actions. This approach helps in building a culture of trust and respect within the team. Inclusive leaders also emphasize collaboration and participation. They understand that the best ideas often emerge from a combination of diverse perspectives and encourage all team members to contribute. This collaborative environment enhances creativity and problem-solving.

Cultural intelligence is another important aspect of inclusive leadership. Leaders with cultural intelligence can effectively bridge the cultural differences within their teams, respecting and leveraging the diverse cultural backgrounds to enhance team performance. Empowerment and support are also central to this leadership style. Inclusive leaders provide their team with the necessary resources, support, and autonomy to succeed, showing a commitment to both professional and personal growth.

Visibility and advocacy for diversity and inclusion within the organization are also key. Inclusive leaders are not just proponents of these values in private but demonstrate their commitment through visible actions and decisions. Adaptability and a commitment to continuous learning are integral to inclusive leadership. Understanding that societal norms and cultural dynamics are fluid, these leaders are always open to learning and evolving their approach to leadership. Inclusive leadership is about creating an environment that values diversity and empowers all employees to contribute and succeed. This leadership approach not only benefits individual team members but also drives the broader innovation and success of the organization.

Cultivating an environment where all team members feel valued and able to contribute is a critical task for any leader, requiring a thoughtful and intentional approach. Leaders should start by creating a culture of open and effective communication. This involves not just speaking but, more importantly, listening. Encouraging team members to share their thoughts and ideas and actively listening to them helps in building trust and shows that their contributions are valued.

Fostering an inclusive culture is also key. This means going beyond just having a diverse team to ensuring that every member feels included and respected. Leaders can achieve this by celebrating different cultures and backgrounds, acknowledging various festivals and holidays, and being mindful of inclusive language. Regular feedback is another important strategy. Providing constructive feedback helps team members understand their strengths and areas for improvement. Recognition of their efforts and accomplishments also plays a significant role in making them feel valued.

Leaders should also focus on equitable distribution of opportunities. This involves giving each team member a chance to lead projects, participate in key meetings, and access professional development resources. Ensuring that opportunities for growth and advancement are available to all is crucial for an equitable environment. Encouraging collaboration and teamwork is essential. Leaders should create opportunities for team members to work together on projects, fostering a sense of camaraderie and mutual support. This not only enhances team spirit but also allows members to learn from each other.

Providing mentorship and support is also valuable. Leaders can pair team members with mentors who can guide them in their career development. This mentorship can be particularly impactful for those who might feel underrepresented or marginalized in the workplace. Leaders should lead by example. Demonstrating inclusivity, respect, and fairness in their actions sets the tone for the rest of the team. When leaders model these behaviors, they create an environment where everyone feels valued and empowered to contribute.

Recognizing and overcoming unconscious biases in leadership decisions and interactions is crucial for fostering a fair and inclusive work environment. Unconscious biases are subtle, often involuntary assumptions and judgments we make about people based on our background, cultural environment, and personal experiences. In leadership, these biases can significantly impact decision-making, interactions, and the overall culture of an organization.

Unconscious biases can manifest in various ways, such as in hiring decisions, promotions, and daily interactions with team members. For instance, a leader might unknowingly favor candidates who share similar backgrounds or experiences, thereby limiting diversity in the team. Similarly, biases can affect how leaders delegate tasks, evaluate performance, and recognize contributions, potentially leading to unequal opportunities and treatment among team members. The impact of not addressing these biases can be profound. It can lead to a workplace where certain groups feel marginalized or undervalued, which can negatively affect morale, productivity, and retention. Moreover, it can hinder the organization's ability to attract diverse talent, as prospective employees seek workplaces that are genuinely inclusive and equitable.

To counter unconscious biases, leaders need to actively engage in self-reflection and education. This involves learning about different types of biases, understanding how they might be influencing one's behavior, and taking steps to mitigate them. Regular bias training sessions for leaders and team members can be effective in raising awareness and providing tools to address these biases.

Implementing structured decision-making processes can also help in minimizing the impact of biases. For instance, using standardized criteria for evaluating candidates during hiring or promotions ensures that decisions are based on objective measures rather than subjective perceptions. Leaders should also seek diverse perspectives and feedback, especially in decision-making. Consulting with a diverse group of individuals can provide a check against biases and lead to more balanced and inclusive decisions. Encouraging a culture of openness and accountability is also important. Leaders should create an environment where team members feel comfortable discussing and pointing out biases, knowing that their concerns will be taken seriously and addressed.

Inclusive Leadership Models

In response to the growing need for more inclusive workplaces, several emerging leadership models have gained prominence. These models emphasize inclusivity, empathy, and collaboration, and are reshaping the traditional notions of leadership.

Servant Leadership

This model is based on the idea of the leader being a 'servant' first, prioritizing the needs of their team members and the organization before their own. Servant leaders focus on empowering and uplifting their teams. They emphasize active listening, empathy, and the personal development of their team members. The goal is to create an environment where employees feel valued, which in turn leads to higher engagement and productivity.

Participative Leadership

Also known as democratic leadership, this model involves leaders who encourage participation and input from all members of the team in decision-making processes. By valuing each team member's perspective and expertise, participative leaders foster a sense of ownership and commitment among their teams. This inclusive approach leads to more diverse ideas, better decision-making, and a more committed and satisfied workforce.

Empathy-Driven Leadership

In this model, empathy is at the core of leadership decisions and interactions. Leaders who adopt this style prioritize understanding and addressing the emotional needs and well-being of their team members. They are skilled at reading emotional cues and adapting their communication and management style accordingly. This empathy-driven approach helps in building strong, trusting relationships within the team, leading to a supportive and cohesive work environment.

Each of these leadership models places a strong emphasis on inclusivity and the well-being of team members. They move away from the traditional top-down approach to leadership, instead fostering environments where collaboration, empathy, and mutual respect are paramount. By adopting these models, leaders can create more inclusive and harmonious workplaces that are conducive to innovation, employee satisfaction, and organizational success.

Several leaders have made significant impacts in their organizations by fostering environments that value diversity, equity, and inclusion. Here are a few notable examples:

Rosie Batty, Luke Batty Foundation

Rosie Batty, an Australian domestic violence campaigner and the founder of the Luke Batty Foundation, is an exemplary inclusive leader. After her personal tragedy, Batty used her voice to advocate for victims of domestic violence. Her leadership style is characterized by empathy, resilience, and the ability to unite people around a cause. Under her guidance, the foundation has made significant strides in raising awareness and changing the conversation around domestic violence in Australia.

Reshma Saujani, Girls Who Code

As the founder of Girls Who Code, Reshma Saujani has been instrumental in closing the gender gap in technology. Her leadership is marked by a passion for promoting diversity and inclusion in the tech industry. Through her organization, Saujani has empowered young women by providing them with the skills and support needed to pursue careers in tech, thus fostering a more inclusive industry.

Doug Conant, Campbell Soup Company

Doug Conant, former CEO of Campbell Soup Company, is known for turning around the company's culture and performance. Conant focused on employee engagement and well-being, believing that a company's success is built on the foundation of a diverse and inclusive workforce. His leadership saw a significant increase in employee satisfaction, which was reflected in the company's improved performance and market reputation.

Alan Joyce, Qantas Airways

Alan Joyce, the CEO of Qantas Airways, has been a proponent of diversity and inclusion, particularly in supporting LGBTQ+ rights. Joyce's leadership has been instrumental in creating an inclusive culture within Qantas, leading to the company being recognized as an employer of choice for LGBTQ+ individuals. His advocacy has also impacted broader societal change, particularly in the realm of marriage equality in Australia.

These leaders exemplify how inclusive leadership can create positive change within organizations and society. Their commitment to inclusivity, empathy, and equity has led to more cohesive work environments, greater innovation, and societal impact, showcasing the profound influence that inclusive leadership can have.

DEI as a Driver for Innovation

A strong focus on Diversity, Equity, and Inclusion (DEI) is increasingly recognized as a key driver of innovation within teams and organizations. When DEI is prioritized, it brings together a rich mix of perspectives, experiences, and skills, which is a fertile ground for innovative thinking and creativity.

Diversity in a team means more than just a collection of different identities; it's about bringing varied life experiences, cultural backgrounds, and ways of thinking into the workplace. This variety ensures that when a team faces a challenge or is brainstorming new ideas, the solutions they come up with are not monolithic but are instead informed by a range of perspectives. Such a diverse team is more likely to identify and creatively solve complex problems, as they are not confined to a single way of thinking.

Equity in the workplace ensures that every team member has an equal opportunity to contribute and be heard. When employees feel that they are treated fairly and their contributions are valued, they are more likely to share their unique ideas and insights. An equitable environment encourages risk-taking and supports employees in pitching novel concepts without fear of bias or discrimination.

Inclusion is the key to unlocking the potential of diverse teams. An inclusive workplace culture not only welcomes diversity but actively engages with it. In such an environment, employees feel comfortable sharing their opinions and experiences. Leaders in inclusive organizations are adept at fostering collaboration and ensuring that all voices are heard and considered. This inclusive culture nurtures a creative and innovative workforce, where new ideas are constantly generated and explored. Organizations that embrace DEI are better equipped to understand and meet the needs of their diverse customer base. The insights gained from a diverse workforce can lead to the development of products and services that appeal to a broader audience, opening up new markets and opportunities for growth.

Fostering a culture that values and leverages diversity for creative problem-solving and innovation is a multifaceted task that requires intentional actions and strategies from leaders. Leaders should start by actively promoting and valuing diversity in all its forms. This goes beyond hiring practices to include nurturing an environment where diverse perspectives are not only welcomed but also sought after. They should ensure that diversity is represented in decision-making bodies and project teams, demonstrating the organization's commitment to diverse viewpoints.

Creating an inclusive culture where every team member feels valued and heard is crucial. Leaders should encourage open dialogue and ensure that all voices are heard in meetings and discussions. This involves not only allowing space for diverse opinions but also actively soliciting input from those who may be less inclined to speak up. It's important for leaders to be aware of and actively work to mitigate unconscious biases. This might involve training for themselves and their teams to understand how biases can influence decision-making and interactions. Leaders should model this awareness in their actions, showing a commitment to fair and unbiased leadership.

Encouraging and facilitating collaboration among team members with diverse backgrounds can lead to more innovative problem-solving. When people with different experiences and viewpoints work together, they can combine their unique perspectives to come up with more creative solutions than homogenous groups. Providing opportunities for continuous learning and exposure to different perspectives is also beneficial. This could include workshops, seminars, or even informal team discussions on topics related to diversity and inclusion. Such learning opportunities can broaden team members' understanding and appreciation of different perspectives.

Recognizing and celebrating diverse contributions can reinforce the value placed on diversity. Leaders should acknowledge and reward creative solutions and innovations that arise from leveraging diverse perspectives. This recognition can motivate the team and reinforce the message that diversity leads to innovation.

Leaders should ensure that the organization's policies and practices support diversity and inclusion. This includes everything from flexible working arrangements to support for professional development for all team members, regardless of their background. By implementing these strategies, leaders can foster a culture that not only values diversity but also leverages it for creative problem-solving and innovation, leading to a more dynamic, creative, and competitive organization.

This chapter has explored the critical role of Diversity, Equity, and Inclusion (DEI) in leadership, emphasizing how these principles are essential for the modern, dynamic workplace. The insights and strategies discussed underscore the importance of integrating DEI into the core fabric of leadership and organizational culture. We highlighted the need for leaders to understand and actively promote diversity in its various forms. This goes beyond demographic diversity to include a mix of backgrounds, experiences, and thought processes. By ensuring diversity in teams and decision-making processes, leaders can harness a wealth of perspectives, leading to enhanced creativity and problem-solving.

Equity was identified as a key component of effective leadership. Ensuring fair treatment, access, opportunity, and advancement for all employees creates a level playing field where every individual can thrive. This includes revising existing policies and practices to eliminate biases and barriers, ensuring equitable access to opportunities, and fostering a culture where each employee's contributions are valued and recognized. Inclusion was also emphasized as a crucial aspect of leadership. Creating an inclusive environment means going beyond just having diverse teams; it involves actively engaging with and valuing the contributions of each team member. Leaders must facilitate open communication, encourage the sharing of diverse opinions, and create a sense of belonging and respect within the team.

The chapter also discussed the need for leaders to be self-aware and continuously educate themselves and their teams about unconscious biases and their impact on decision-making and team dynamics. Leaders must lead by example, demonstrating inclusivity in their actions and decisions. We also pointed out the benefits of leveraging diversity for innovation. By encouraging collaboration among diverse team members and creating an environment where different perspectives are valued, leaders can drive creativity and innovation within their teams.

As we conclude our exploration of Diversity, Equity, and Inclusion (DEI) in leadership, we pave the way to our next chapter, which delves into the evolving role of technology in leadership. The principles of DEI, with their emphasis on inclusive and adaptive practices, set the stage for understanding how technology is reshaping leadership in the modern era.

In the upcoming chapter, we will explore how technological advancements are influencing leadership styles, communication, decision-making, and overall team dynamics. We'll examine the challenges and opportunities that arise from integrating technology in leadership practices, especially in terms of maintaining inclusivity and equity in increasingly digital work environments. The intersection of technology and leadership opens up new avenues for innovation, collaboration, and productivity. As we transition into this new chapter, we will uncover how leaders can leverage technology to enhance their effectiveness while staying true to the principles of DEI, ensuring that technology is used as a tool to support and advance these critical values in their organizations.

7. Technology-Driven Leadership

The purpose of this chapter is to delve into the integration of technology in leadership, with a specific focus on how it influences decision-making and enhances efficiency. In an era where technology is rapidly evolving and becoming increasingly integral to everyday business operations, understanding its impact on leadership is crucial.

We will explore how various technological tools and platforms are transforming the way leaders make decisions. From data analytics to artificial intelligence, technology offers new insights and capabilities that can lead to more informed, timely, and effective decision-making processes. This part of the chapter will examine the benefits and challenges of relying on technology for decision-making, including how to balance data-driven insights with human judgment. The chapter will discuss how technology can streamline operations and increase efficiency in leadership roles. We will look at tools and software that automate routine tasks, facilitate communication, and manage workflows, freeing up leaders to focus on more strategic aspects of their roles.

The chapter will also consider the implications of these technological integrations for team dynamics and organizational culture. It will address the skills and competencies that leaders need to effectively manage technology-augmented teams and how to ensure that technology serves to enhance rather than hinder team performance and employee engagement.

The rise of technology in the modern workplace has fundamentally reshaped the landscape of leadership. In an era where digital transformation is no longer a choice but a necessity, technology has become a crucial component in guiding organizational strategy, operations, and culture.

Today's leaders are navigating a world where technological advancements are rapidly evolving, influencing every aspect of business. The integration of digital tools and platforms into daily operations has become essential for maintaining competitiveness and relevance in a global market. From cloud computing and big data analytics to artificial intelligence (AI) and the Internet of Things (IoT), technology is changing the way organizations operate, make decisions, and interact with their customers and employees.

The impact of technology on communication cannot be overstated. Digital communication tools have revolutionized how leaders connect with their teams, enabling real-time collaboration across different geographies and time zones. This shift has been particularly crucial in the wake of the COVID-19 pandemic, where remote work has become the norm, challenging leaders to maintain team cohesion and productivity in a virtual environment.

Technology has transformed the decision-making process. Access to vast amounts of data and advanced analytical tools allows leaders to gain deeper insights, predict trends, and make more informed decisions. This data-driven approach can lead to more strategic and effective leadership, as decisions are based on concrete information rather than intuition.

With these advancements come new challenges. Leaders must now grapple with issues such as cybersecurity, digital ethics, and the digital divide. They need to develop skills to manage a technologically advanced workplace, including understanding the basics of new technologies, leading remote and technologically augmented teams, and ensuring that technology is used ethically and responsibly.

The Role of Data Analytics in Leadership

Data analytics, a critical component in the modern organizational toolkit, refers to the process of examining data sets to draw conclusions about the information they contain. This process, increasingly powered by specialized systems and software, allows leaders to analyze and interpret complex data to inform decision-making, uncover patterns, identify trends, and make predictions.

The growing importance of data analytics in organizational decision-making stems from its ability to turn vast amounts of raw data into actionable insights. In today's data-driven world, organizations accumulate a staggering amount of information from various sources - customer interactions, sales transactions, online activities, and more. Data analytics enables leaders to sift through this information and extract relevant insights that can guide strategic planning, operational improvements, and market positioning.

Data analytics comes in various forms, including descriptive analytics, which looks at past performance to understand what happened; predictive analytics, which models and forecasts future possibilities; and prescriptive analytics, which suggests actions to achieve desired outcomes. Each type plays a crucial role in providing a comprehensive view of an organization's performance and future opportunities.

For leaders, the ability to leverage data analytics is becoming increasingly essential. It offers a more objective basis for decision-making, minimizing biases and assumptions that can affect human judgment. Data-driven insights can lead to better resource allocation, more effective marketing strategies, improved customer experiences, and ultimately, a stronger competitive edge in the marketplace. Data analytics is pivotal in identifying inefficiencies and areas for improvement within an organization. It can help leaders pinpoint operational bottlenecks, optimize processes, and enhance productivity, leading to cost savings and improved performance.

Data-driven decision-making marks a significant shift in how leaders approach strategy, operations, and problem-solving. By leveraging data analytics, leaders can base their decisions on empirical evidence, leading to more accurate and effective outcomes. Using data analytics, leaders can gain deep insights into various aspects of their business. For example, customer data can reveal preferences and behaviors, helping to tailor products or services to meet market needs. Similarly, internal data such as sales figures, employee performance metrics, and operational efficiencies can highlight areas for improvement or investment.

One of the primary benefits of a data-driven approach is the ability to make decisions that are not solely based on intuition or experience. While these traditional factors are important, combining them with concrete data provides a more holistic view. This method reduces biases and assumptions, leading to more objective and rational decision-making. Data analytics also enables predictive capabilities. By analyzing trends and patterns, leaders can anticipate market changes, customer needs, or potential operational issues before they become problematic. This foresight allows for proactive strategies, rather than reactive measures, giving organizations a competitive edge. Data-driven strategies can lead to increased efficiency and cost savings. Analyzing operational data helps identify inefficiencies or bottlenecks, allowing leaders to optimize processes and allocate resources more effectively. This can lead to significant cost reductions and improved organizational performance.

In an era where the business landscape is constantly evolving, the ability to quickly adapt strategies based on real-time data is invaluable. Data analytics provides leaders with the agility to pivot and respond to changing market conditions, customer feedback, or internal challenges swiftly and effectively. The integration of data analytics into decision-making processes enables leaders to make more informed, efficient, and effective decisions. This data-driven approach not only enhances the accuracy of decisions but also provides a robust foundation for strategic planning and operational management.

While data-driven decision-making offers numerous advantages, it also comes with its own set of challenges. Relying on data for critical decisions requires careful consideration of various factors, including data quality, interpretation errors, and ethical considerations.

One significant challenge is ensuring the quality of the data. Poor quality data, which can be due to inaccuracies, incompleteness, or outdated information, can lead to misleading insights. Organizations must establish robust processes for data collection, validation, and maintenance to ensure that the data they rely on for decision-making is accurate and reliable.

Interpretation errors present another challenge. Data can be complex, and its interpretation requires a certain level of expertise. Misinterpreting data can lead to incorrect conclusions and poor decisions. This risk underscores the importance of having skilled data analysts and ensuring that leaders have a good understanding of data analytics principles. Additionally, it's crucial to approach data interpretation within the broader context of the business environment and market trends.

Ethical considerations are also paramount when relying on data. This includes concerns about privacy, especially when handling sensitive personal data of customers or employees. Leaders must navigate the legal and ethical implications of data use, ensuring compliance with data protection regulations and maintaining the trust of stakeholders. Another ethical aspect relates to bias in data. Algorithms and data models can inadvertently perpetuate existing biases, leading to decisions that may be unfair or discriminatory. Leaders need to be aware of these potential biases and actively work to mitigate them. This might involve diverse data sets, regular reviews of data models, and incorporating ethical considerations into data analysis processes.

There's the risk of over-reliance on data. While data is a powerful tool, it should not be the only factor in decision-making. Leaders need to balance data insights with human judgment and consider factors that may not be immediately apparent in the data. While data-driven decision-making is a powerful approach, it requires careful management of data quality, skilled interpretation, and ethical consideration. Leaders must be cognizant of these challenges and take proactive steps to address them, ensuring that their reliance on data leads to fair, ethical, and effective decisions. Integrating Data Analytics into Leadership Practices

Data analytics, with its far-reaching implications, can be practically applied in various leadership scenarios, offering insights that drive strategic decisions and operational efficiency. In strategic planning, data analytics can be a game-changer. Leaders can use data to identify market trends, customer preferences, and emerging industry shifts. For instance, by analyzing consumer behavior and sales data, a company can pinpoint which products are performing well and which are not, helping to inform future product development and investment decisions. Predictive analytics can also forecast future market trends, enabling leaders to strategize accordingly.

In the realm of marketing, data analytics is indispensable. It allows leaders to understand customer demographics, behaviors, and preferences in depth. By analyzing data from various sources like social media, website traffic, and customer surveys, marketing teams can tailor their strategies to target specific customer segments more effectively. This data-driven approach can significantly improve the return on investment for marketing campaigns by ensuring that they resonate with the intended audience. Human resource management is another area where data analytics plays a crucial role. Leaders can use data to optimize recruitment processes, identify skills gaps in their current workforce, and understand employee satisfaction and engagement levels. For example, analyzing employee performance data can help identify high performers who may be suitable for leadership roles, aiding succession planning. Data analytics can also be used to analyze patterns in employee turnover, helping leaders understand why employees may be leaving and what steps can be taken to improve retention.

In operations management, data analytics can streamline processes and improve efficiency. Leaders can analyze operational data to identify bottlenecks or inefficiencies in their processes. For instance, in a manufacturing context, data analysis can reveal inefficiencies in the production line, which can then be addressed to reduce waste and increase productivity. In financial management, leaders can use data analytics for budgeting, forecasting, and financial planning. Analyzing financial trends and historical data helps in making more accurate predictions about future revenue and expenditure, allowing for more informed budgetary decisions.

In today's data-driven business environment, several key tools and technologies facilitate data analytics in leadership. These tools enable leaders to harness the power of data for making informed decisions, identifying trends, and driving organizational success.

Artificial Intelligence (AI)

AI plays a pivotal role in data analytics by enabling the processing and analysis of vast amounts of data at incredible speeds. AI algorithms can detect patterns and insights that might be impossible for humans to discern, providing leaders with a deeper understanding of business operations, customer behavior, and market trends.

Machine Learning (ML)

A subset of AI, machine learning involves algorithms that learn from data and improve over time. ML can be particularly useful in predictive analytics, where it helps in forecasting future trends based on historical data. For example, ML can predict customer buying patterns, helping leaders make strategic decisions in marketing and sales.

Business Intelligence (BI) Platforms

BI platforms like Tableau, Microsoft Power BI, and SAS Business Intelligence provide comprehensive tools for data visualization and analysis. These platforms allow leaders to convert raw data into easy-to-understand charts, graphs, and dashboards, facilitating quick and effective decision-making. They often include features for reporting, online analytical processing, analytics, dashboard development, and data mining.

Big Data Analytics Tools

Tools like Apache Hadoop and Spark are designed to handle massive volumes of data - known as big data. These tools are essential for organizations dealing with large-scale data sets, enabling them to store, process, and analyze data efficiently. They are particularly useful in uncovering insights from unstructured data, such as social media content, emails, and documents.

Cloud Computing

Cloud-based analytics tools have revolutionized data analytics by providing scalable, flexible, and cost-effective solutions. Cloud platforms like Amazon Web Services (AWS), Google Cloud, and Microsoft Azure offer a range of services for storing, processing, and analyzing data. They provide the advantage of accessing powerful computing resources on-demand, without the need for significant upfront investment in infrastructure.

Customer Relationship Management (CRM) Systems

Modern CRM systems like Salesforce and HubSpot come equipped with analytics features that help leaders understand customer interactions and preferences. These systems provide valuable insights into customer behavior, sales trends, and campaign effectiveness, enabling leaders to make data-driven decisions in customer service and marketing strategies.

These tools and technologies are essential for leaders in the digital age, providing them with the capabilities to make informed decisions, stay ahead of market trends, and drive organizational success through data-driven strategies.

Technology in Enhancing Efficiency and Productivity

Technological tools and software have become indispensable in enhancing organizational efficiency. These tools streamline operations, facilitate communication, and automate routine tasks, allowing organizations to operate more effectively and focus on strategic goals.

Project management software like Asana, Trello, and Microsoft Project plays a crucial role in organizing and tracking the progress of various projects. These platforms provide features like task assignments, deadline tracking, and progress updates, helping teams stay on track and collaborate effectively. They also offer visual representations of projects, making it easier for leaders to monitor progress and allocate resources efficiently.

Communication tools have revolutionized how teams interact and collaborate. Platforms such as Slack, Microsoft Teams, and Zoom enable real-time communication and collaboration, regardless of geographical location. They support a range of functionalities from instant messaging and video conferencing to file sharing and collaborative document editing. These tools are particularly valuable in maintaining connectivity and productivity in remote or hybrid work environments. Automation technologies are transforming how organizations handle repetitive and time-consuming tasks. Tools like Zapier, UiPath, and Automation Anywhere allow for the automation of various administrative and operational processes, from scheduling and email responses to more complex tasks like data entry and report generation. By automating these tasks, organizations can reduce human error, save time, and increase overall efficiency.

Customer Relationship Management (CRM) systems, such as Salesforce and HubSpot, streamline customer management and interactions. These systems automate and organize customer communications, sales tracking, and marketing efforts, providing comprehensive insights into customer behavior and improving the effectiveness of sales and marketing strategies. Cloud computing services, including Amazon Web Services (AWS), Google Cloud, and Microsoft Azure, offer scalable and flexible resources for data storage, processing, and analysis. They provide the advantage of accessing powerful computing capabilities and large storage capacities without the need for significant physical infrastructure, enhancing organizational agility and efficiency.

These technological tools and software are pivotal in modern organizations. They enable efficient project management, seamless communication, automation of routine tasks, effective customer relationship management, and flexible computing resources, all of which contribute to increased organizational efficiency and productivity.

Several organizations across various industries have successfully leveraged technology to boost productivity and efficiency, demonstrating the transformative power of digital tools in the business world.

Toyota and Lean Manufacturing

Toyota is renowned for its implementation of lean manufacturing principles, significantly aided by technology. The company's use of automation and robotics in its production lines has dramatically increased efficiency. Toyota's Just-in-Time system (JIT), a key component of its lean manufacturing approach, relies heavily on technology to ensure materials are only ordered and received as needed, reducing waste and increasing efficiency.

Netflix and Cloud Computing

Netflix's transition to cloud computing is a prime example of leveraging technology for efficiency. By moving its operations to Amazon Web Services (AWS), Netflix significantly improved its streaming quality and speed while managing to scale up or down based on demand. This shift not only enhanced user experience but also optimized costs and operational efficiency.

Zara and Fast Fashion

The fashion retailer Zara has effectively used technology to revolutionize the fast fashion industry. By using advanced data analytics and inventory management systems, Zara can quickly respond to changing fashion trends. This agility allows them to bring new designs from concept to store shelves in just a few weeks, significantly faster than traditional fashion retailers.
Walmart and Data Analytics

Walmart employs sophisticated data analytics to optimize its supply chain and inventory management. The company analyzes massive amounts of data from its stores to predict buying trends, manage stock levels, and optimize logistics. This data-driven approach has enabled Walmart to reduce costs and improve customer satisfaction by ensuring products are always in stock.

American Express and Predictive Analytics

American Express uses predictive analytics to provide personalized services to its customers and prevent fraud. By analyzing transaction data, American Express can identify spending patterns and detect unusual activity that may indicate fraud. This proactive approach not only protects customers but also enhances their experience by tailoring services to their needs.

These case studies demonstrate how technology can be a powerful enabler of productivity and efficiency. From manufacturing and retail to services and entertainment, the strategic application of technology can lead to significant performance improvements and a competitive edge in the marketplace.

Leadership in the Age of Digital Transformation

Navigating digital transformation is a complex and critical task for modern leaders. It requires a combination of strategic vision, effective change management, and a focus on employee engagement.

Strategic Vision

Leaders play a crucial role in setting the strategic vision for digital transformation. This vision should align with the organization's overall goals and objectives, providing a clear direction for the digital journey. Leaders must understand the potential of digital technologies and how they can be harnessed to enhance business processes, improve customer experiences, and drive innovation. By articulating a compelling digital vision, leaders can inspire their teams and stakeholders to embrace the transformation.

Change Management

Digital transformation often involves significant changes in processes, systems, and even organizational culture. Effective change management is essential to navigate this transition successfully. Leaders must plan and implement the transformation in a way that minimizes disruption and maximizes acceptance. This involves clear communication about the benefits and impact of the transformation, addressing concerns and resistance, and providing the necessary resources and support. Leaders must also be adaptable, ready to adjust strategies in response to challenges and new opportunities that arise during the transformation journey.

Employee Engagement

For digital transformation to be successful, employee buy-in and engagement are crucial. Leaders must ensure that employees understand the importance of the transformation and how it benefits them and the organization. Training and development play a key role here, equipping employees with the skills and knowledge needed to thrive in a digitally transformed workplace. Leaders should also foster a culture of innovation and experimentation, encouraging employees to contribute ideas and be part of the transformation process.

Fostering a culture that embraces technological advancements and continuous learning is essential for organizations looking to thrive in the digital era. Leaders play a pivotal role in cultivating this culture.

Leaders should start by setting a clear example of embracing technology and learning. When leaders are seen actively using new technologies and investing in their own learning, it sets a powerful precedent for the rest of the organization. They should demonstrate not only how to use these technologies but also their benefits and impact on the organization's goals. Communication is key in fostering this culture. Leaders need to clearly and effectively communicate the importance and benefits of embracing technology and continuous learning. This involves not just talking about the "what" and the "how" but also the "why" behind these technological changes. Understanding the rationale behind technology adoption makes employees more likely to embrace it.

Creating opportunities for learning and development is also crucial. This could involve providing training sessions, workshops, or online courses for employees to learn about new technologies and how they can be applied in their work. Leaders should encourage and facilitate participation in these learning opportunities. Encouraging a mindset of experimentation and innovation is important. Leaders should create an environment where employees feel safe to experiment with new technologies, make mistakes, and learn from them. This can involve setting up innovation labs or hackathons, or simply encouraging employees to try out new technologies in their projects.

Recognizing and rewarding employees who embrace technology and learning can reinforce this culture. Leaders can acknowledge and reward teams that successfully implement new technologies or come up with innovative solutions. This not only motivates employees but also shows that the organization values these initiatives. Leaders should ensure that the organization's policies and infrastructure support the adoption of technology and learning. This includes investing in the necessary technological tools and ensuring that employees have access to the resources they need to learn and experiment with new technologies.

By implementing these strategies, leaders can create an organizational culture that not only embraces technological advancements but also sees continuous learning as a key component of professional development and organizational success.

Ethical Considerations in Technology-Driven Leadership

The ethical use of technology and data in leadership is a critical area of concern in the digital age. As leaders increasingly rely on technology and data analytics for decision-making, they must navigate a range of ethical considerations to ensure responsible and fair use. One of the primary ethical considerations is the privacy of individuals, especially when handling personal data. Leaders need to ensure that data collection and processing are done in compliance with privacy laws and regulations, like the General Data Protection Regulation (GDPR). They must also respect individual privacy rights and ensure that personal data is used in a way that is transparent and consensual.

With the increasing reliance on digital technologies, the risk of data breaches and cyber attacks has escalated. Leaders must prioritize data security to protect sensitive information from unauthorized access and cyber threats. This involves investing in robust cybersecurity measures, regularly updating security protocols, and training employees on data security best practices.

Another significant ethical issue is the potential for bias in data and technology. Algorithms and data sets can inadvertently perpetuate existing biases, leading to unfair or discriminatory outcomes. Leaders must be aware of these potential biases and actively work to mitigate them. This can involve using diverse data sets, regularly reviewing and updating algorithms, and implementing checks and balances to ensure fairness and accuracy in data-driven decisions.

As artificial intelligence (AI) and automation technologies become more prevalent, leaders must consider the ethical implications of their use. This includes the impact on employment, the potential for misuse, and the need for transparency in how AI-driven decisions are made. Leaders should strive to use AI and automation in ways that enhance human work and productivity, rather than replace it, and ensure that these technologies are used responsibly and ethically.

Ethical leadership in the digital age also demands transparency and accountability in the use of technology and data. Leaders should be clear about how and why they are using technology and data and be accountable for the outcomes of these decisions. This involves open communication with stakeholders and a commitment to addressing any issues or concerns that arise.

Ethical considerations in the use of technology and data are complex and multifaceted. Leaders must navigate these challenges carefully, ensuring that they respect privacy, prioritize data security, mitigate biases, use AI and automation responsibly, and maintain transparency and accountability in their digital practices. By doing so, they can harness the power of technology and data in a way that is ethical, responsible, and aligned with the values of their organization and society. Developing and implementing ethical guidelines for technology use in leadership involves a series of thoughtful and intentional actions. Initially, it is crucial to assess and understand the ethical landscape surrounding the technologies used or planned for use within the organization. This understanding should encompass various aspects like privacy, data security, potential biases, and other ethical concerns that might arise from technology use.

Following this assessment, leaders should establish a set of clear ethical principles that align with the organization's core values. These principles should address specific concerns such as respecting user privacy, ensuring data security, and maintaining fairness in algorithmic processes. The establishment of these principles is the foundation for guiding ethical technology use.

Involving a diverse group of stakeholders in the development of these guidelines is essential. Including IT professionals, legal advisors, HR, and representatives from various departments ensures that the guidelines are comprehensive and take into account different perspectives and impacts across the organization. Translating these ethical principles into specific, actionable policies and procedures is the next critical step. This could include guidelines on responsible data collection and usage, protocols for AI and machine learning applications, and procedures for handling data breaches.

To ensure these policies are effectively integrated into the organization, implementing training and awareness programs for all employees is necessary. Such programs should educate employees on the ethical use of technology, the organization's specific guidelines, and the role each employee plays in upholding these standards. Regular training is important to keep pace with the evolving nature of technology and ethical considerations.

It's vital to regularly monitor and review these ethical guidelines. As technology evolves, so too do its ethical implications. Regular reviews and updates of the guidelines are necessary to stay current and address new challenges and legal requirements. Promoting a culture of ethical technology use within the organization is imperative. Leaders need to lead by example, openly discuss the importance of ethical technology use, and recognize and reward behaviors that align with the ethical guidelines. This creates an environment where ethical use of technology is part of the organizational ethos.

By undertaking these steps, leaders can ensure that the integration of technology within their organizations is conducted in a responsible manner, aligning with both the organization's values and the broader ethical standards of society. This approach not only mitigates risks but also builds trust and integrity within the organization and among external stakeholders.

Preparing for Future Technological Advancements

Emerging technologies are set to have a profound impact on leadership in the near future, reshaping how leaders manage operations, make decisions, and interact with their teams.

Augmented Reality (AR)

Augmented reality, which overlays digital information onto the physical world, is poised to transform various aspects of business and leadership. In training and development, for example, AR can provide immersive and interactive experiences, making learning more engaging and effective. It can also be used in product design and development, allowing leaders and teams to visualize and interact with 3D models in real-time, enhancing creativity and innovation.

Blockchain

Known primarily for its application in cryptocurrencies, blockchain technology has far-reaching implications beyond finance. Its ability to provide secure, transparent, and tamper-proof records makes it valuable for supply chain management, contract execution, and secure data sharing. Leaders in industries ranging from healthcare to manufacturing are exploring blockchain's potential to streamline operations and ensure data integrity.

Advanced AI

Artificial intelligence continues to evolve, with advanced AI systems capable of more sophisticated tasks and decision-making. These systems can analyze large datasets to identify trends and insights, assist in strategic planning, and even automate complex decision-making processes. The challenge for leaders will be to integrate advanced AI into their operations effectively while addressing ethical concerns and ensuring a human-centric approach.

Internet of Things (IoT)

The IoT, which connects everyday devices to the internet, is enabling more data-driven decision-making. For leaders, the IoT offers insights into everything from consumer behavior to operational efficiency. In the future, IoT could lead to more connected, responsive, and smart business environments, where leaders can monitor and manage operations remotely and in real-time.

These emerging technologies present both opportunities and challenges for leaders. While they offer the potential to drive innovation and efficiency, leaders must also navigate issues related to integration, employee training, privacy, and ethical use.

Staying abreast of these technologies and understanding their implications will be crucial for effective leadership in the coming years.

In today's rapidly evolving digital landscape, the ability for leaders to engage in continuous learning and adaptation is not just advantageous but essential. Staying current with technological advancements is crucial for maintaining relevance, competitiveness, and effectiveness in leadership. The pace at which new technologies are developed and adopted has accelerated, dramatically transforming business models, operational processes, and market dynamics. Leaders who fail to keep up with these changes risk falling behind, making their organizations less competitive and potentially obsolete. Therefore, embracing a mindset of continuous learning is critical. This involves staying informed about emerging technologies such as AI, blockchain, and IoT, and understanding their potential impact on the industry and organization.

Continuous learning enables leaders to foresee and adapt to technological disruptions. By understanding the trends and directions of technological advancements, leaders can anticipate changes and strategically position their organizations to leverage new opportunities. This proactive approach to technology adoption can lead to innovation, improved efficiency, and better customer experiences.

Adaptation is equally important in this journey. As new technologies emerge, leaders must be willing to adapt their strategies and operations. This might involve investing in new technologies, retraining staff, or even altering the organization's business model. Leaders need to be agile, flexible, and open to change to successfully navigate the digital transformation.

Staying current with technology is vital for attracting and retaining talent. The modern workforce, especially younger generations, expects to work in an environment that embraces technological advancements. Leaders who demonstrate a commitment to leveraging the latest technologies are more likely to attract innovative and tech-savvy employees.

Leaders must also cultivate a culture within their organizations that values and encourages continuous learning and adaptation. This could involve providing training and development opportunities, encouraging experimentation and innovation, and fostering an environment where learning from failures is seen as a valuable part of growth.

This chapter has delved into the critical role of technology in modern leadership, exploring various aspects and strategies for effectively integrating technology into leadership practices. The chapter began by setting the stage for the rise of technology in the modern workplace, highlighting how technological advancements have become integral to leadership. From streamlining operations to enhancing communication, technology is reshaping the way leaders manage and guide their organizations. We then explored the concept of data analytics and its growing importance in organizational decision-making. Leaders can use data analytics to inform their strategies, gaining insights that drive more informed and effective decision-making processes. The benefits of a data-driven approach were discussed, emphasizing how it leads to better strategic planning, marketing decisions, and human resource management.

The potential challenges of relying on data, such as issues with data quality, interpretation errors, and ethical considerations, were also addressed. Leaders need to be cognizant of these challenges and take proactive steps to ensure the ethical and accurate use of data. Practical applications of data analytics in various leadership scenarios were presented, showcasing how data can inform decisions in areas like strategic planning, marketing, and human resources. This illustrated the versatility and impact of data analytics in driving organizational success.

The chapter also reviewed key tools and technologies that facilitate data analytics, including AI, machine learning, and business intelligence platforms. These technologies are essential for leaders in the digital age, enabling them to make informed decisions, stay ahead of market trends, and drive organizational success. We highlighted the importance of continuous learning and adaptation for leaders. In an era where technology is rapidly evolving, leaders must stay informed about technological advancements and be willing to adapt their strategies and operations accordingly. This continuous learning and adaptability are key to maintaining relevance and competitiveness in the digital era.

Integrating technology into leadership is essential for navigating the complexities of the modern business landscape. By leveraging data analytics, staying abreast of technological advancements, and embracing continuous learning and adaptability, leaders can enhance their effectiveness and guide their organizations to greater success.

As we transition from exploring the integration of technology in leadership, our focus shifts to the next chapter, where we delve into global leadership challenges in multicultural settings. The concepts of technology-driven leadership provide a seamless segue into this new area of discussion, as technology is a key enabler for leaders operating in diverse and globally dispersed environments.

The next chapter will explore the intricacies of leading across different cultures and geographies, a challenge accentuated in today's interconnected world. We will examine how the technological skills and strategies discussed previously can be leveraged to navigate the complexities of global leadership. This includes using technology to bridge geographical and cultural gaps, facilitate communication, and foster understanding and collaboration in diverse teams. We will look at the unique challenges posed by multicultural settings, such as managing cross-cultural communication, adapting leadership styles to different cultural norms, and building cohesive teams with diverse backgrounds. The chapter will provide insights into how leaders can effectively harness technology to overcome these challenges and lead successfully in a global context.

8. Global Leadership in Multicultural Settings

In today's increasingly globalized business world, leaders face a myriad of unique challenges that stem from operating across diverse cultural, economic, and regulatory environments. The globalization of business has expanded dramatically, driven by advancements in technology, communication, and transportation. Markets are more interconnected than ever, with businesses operating across borders and reaching customers in every corner of the globe. This interconnectedness, while creating vast opportunities, also presents a set of challenges for leadership.

One of the key challenges is navigating cultural diversity. Global leaders must understand and respect the cultural nuances and business practices of different regions. This requires a deep appreciation of how culture influences communication styles, decision-making processes, and workplace dynamics.

Another challenge is managing geographically dispersed teams. Leaders must find ways to foster collaboration, cohesion, and a shared sense of purpose among team members who may be spread across various time zones and locations. This involves overcoming language barriers and using technology effectively to maintain communication and workflow. Global leaders must navigate varying legal and regulatory environments. Each country or region has its own set of laws and business regulations, and leaders must ensure their organizations comply with these local requirements while maintaining consistent global standards.

Economic volatility and political uncertainty in different regions also add to the complexity. Leaders must be adept at adapting strategies in response to changing economic conditions and geopolitical shifts to mitigate risks and capitalize on opportunities. The global leadership landscape presents a challenging but rewarding arena. Leaders who can effectively navigate these complexities are well-positioned to take advantage of the opportunities presented by a globalized business environment.

This chapter will delve deeper into these challenges and explore strategies for successful global leadership. We will examine how leaders can effectively communicate, build trust, and foster collaboration in multicultural teams, understanding and bridging cultural differences to create cohesive and productive work environments. The chapter will also address the challenges of leading in various international contexts, including adapting to local business practices, regulatory environments, and navigating geopolitical dynamics.

By the end of this chapter, readers will gain insights into how to lead effectively in multicultural and international settings, equipping them with the knowledge to harness the strengths of diversity and drive global business success.

Understanding Multicultural Leadership

Multicultural leadership is a critical concept in today's increasingly interconnected and globalized business environment. This form of leadership refers to the ability to effectively manage and lead culturally diverse teams, acknowledging and leveraging the richness that different backgrounds, perspectives, and experiences bring to an organization. The importance of multicultural leadership stems from the growing diversity in the workforce and the expansion of businesses into new global markets. Leaders in multicultural environments face the unique challenge of bridging cultural divides, aligning individuals with different cultural values and work practices towards common organizational goals.

Effective multicultural leadership involves more than just an awareness of cultural differences. It requires an in-depth understanding of how these differences can affect communication, teamwork, and employee motivation. Multicultural leaders must possess strong intercultural communication skills, showing sensitivity and adaptability to various cultural norms and expectations.

Such leaders play a crucial role in creating an inclusive environment where all team members feel valued and understood. This inclusivity is key to fostering mutual respect and collaboration in diverse teams. When team members from different cultural backgrounds feel their perspectives are respected and their contributions valued, it leads to greater innovation, problem-solving, and overall team performance. Multicultural leadership is about embracing and celebrating diversity, not just as a moral imperative but as a strategic advantage. Leaders who excel in multicultural environments are able to harness the diverse talents and insights of their teams, leading to more effective and innovative organizational outcomes.

Leaders in multicultural environments often face a unique set of challenges, which can impact team dynamics, communication, and overall effectiveness. Understanding and addressing these challenges is crucial for successful leadership.

Cultural Misunderstandings

One of the primary challenges is navigating cultural misunderstandings. Different cultures have varying norms, values, and business practices, which can lead to misinterpretations or conflicts. For example, what is considered a straightforward communication style in one culture might be perceived as rude or disrespectful in another. Leaders must be culturally sensitive and aware, taking the time to understand the cultural backgrounds of their team members to avoid misunderstandings.

Communication Barriers

Effective communication can be challenging in multicultural settings, especially when language differences are involved. Even when a common language is used, nuances and non-verbal cues can be misunderstood. Leaders must be adept at clear and inclusive communication, often relying on visual aids, simplifying language, and ensuring that key messages are understood by all team members.

Managing Diverse Perspectives

Multicultural teams bring a variety of perspectives and approaches to problem-solving and decision-making. While this diversity can be a significant asset, it can also lead to challenges in reaching consensus or in decision-making processes. Leaders need to balance these diverse viewpoints, ensuring that all voices are heard and considered. This requires strong facilitation skills and the ability to manage conflicts constructively.

Balancing Integration and Individuality

Leaders must find the right balance between creating a cohesive team culture and respecting individual cultural identities. Overemphasis on assimilation can lead to a loss of unique perspectives, while too much focus on individuality can hinder team unity. Leaders should strive to create an environment where individual cultural identities are celebrated and integrated into the broader team and organizational culture.

Adapting Leadership Styles

Effective leadership in multicultural environments often requires adapting one's leadership style to suit different cultural norms and expectations. A leadership approach that works well in one cultural context may not be effective in another. Leaders must be flexible and adaptable, modifying their approach as needed to suit the cultural context of their team members.

Building Trust Across Cultures

Establishing trust can be particularly challenging in multicultural environments due to different cultural norms and expectations regarding trust-building. Leaders need to understand these differences and work to build trust through consistent, respectful, and fair interactions.

The merger of Roche and Genentech offers a compelling example of the complexities and triumphs of multicultural leadership in action. When the Swiss pharmaceutical giant Roche acquired the U.S.-based biotechnology firm Genentech in 2009, it wasn't just a union of two companies but a fusion of two distinct corporate cultures and management styles. Roche's structured, hierarchical approach contrasted sharply with Genentech's informal, collaborative ethos, reflective of Silicon Valley's entrepreneurial spirit.

One of the foremost challenges in this merger was the integration of these differing cultures. Genentech's employees harbored concerns about losing their unique and cherished company culture, which was seen as a cornerstone of their innovation and success. Meanwhile, Roche was tasked with ensuring that the combined entity functioned cohesively and adhered to its broader organizational objectives.

The merger's success is largely attributed to the leadership approaches at both Roche and Genentech. Leaders from both sides committed themselves to a path of open communication, mutual respect for each company's strengths, and a dedication to finding a common ground that would benefit the merged entity. They recognized the importance of preserving Genentech's innovative culture while seamlessly blending the two companies. The outcome of the Roche-Genentech merger stands as a testament to successful multicultural leadership. The integrated company has continued to lead in the biotechnology and pharmaceutical sectors, striking a balance where Genentech's pioneering spirit thrives within Roche's global structure.

A key strategy that contributed to the success of the merger was the respect shown for Genentech's unique culture. Roche's leadership recognized the value of Genentech's collaborative and innovative environment and actively sought to preserve it, rather than impose its own corporate culture. This approach played a crucial role in alleviating fears among Genentech's employees about losing their distinctive work culture. Another significant aspect of the merger's success was the emphasis on effective communication. Roche ensured open and transparent communication throughout the process, keeping lines open and maintaining clarity about the objectives and processes of the merger. This approach was instrumental in building trust, reducing uncertainties, and minimizing resistance among the workforce.

The balanced integration approach taken by Roche was also a key factor in the merger's success. Roche struck a fine balance between integrating Genentech into its global operations and allowing it to retain some degree of autonomy. This strategy ensured operational cohesion while maintaining Genentech's unique strengths and capabilities.

The merger was not without its challenges. Initially, there were significant concerns among Genentech's staff about the potential loss of their company culture. This apprehension could have led to decreased morale and talent loss had it not been carefully managed. Additionally, aligning the different business practices and operational procedures of the two companies was a complex task that required meticulous planning and execution.

From the Roche-Genentech merger, several key lessons can be drawn. The importance of cultural sensitivity in mergers and acquisitions is paramount. Recognizing and valuing the culture of an acquired company can significantly impact the success of the integration. Clear and consistent communication throughout the merger process is vital in managing employee expectations and reducing resistance to change. Furthermore, the value of a strategic integration approach that balances cohesion with respect for individuality is crucial. This approach allows for leveraging synergies while preserving the unique attributes that make each company successful. Lastly, actively engaging employees in the process and addressing their concerns can mitigate fears and foster a sense of unity and purpose.

Strategies for Global Leadership

Cultural Intelligence (CQ) is a critical competency in today's globalized business environment, especially for leaders who navigate diverse cultural landscapes. CQ refers to the capability to relate and work effectively across cultures, and it's an essential skill for global leaders to effectively manage multicultural teams, negotiate international deals, and adapt business strategies to different cultural contexts. Leaders with high CQ are more successful in bridging the diversity gap, leading to improved communication, stronger team cohesion, and enhanced overall performance. They are adept at understanding and respecting different cultural norms and practices, which helps in building trust and credibility with team members and business partners from various cultural backgrounds.

Developing CQ involves several strategies:

1. Education and Awareness: One of the first steps in developing CQ is education. Leaders should actively seek to learn about different cultures, their values, beliefs, and business practices. This can be achieved through formal training, workshops, or self-study. Gaining a foundational understanding of different cultural dimensions helps leaders anticipate and navigate cultural differences.

2. Experiential Learning: Real-world exposure to different cultures is invaluable. This can include traveling, working in international settings, or engaging in cross-cultural projects. Experiential learning allows leaders to immerse themselves in different cultures, providing practical insights and a deeper understanding of cultural nuances.

3. Reflective Practices: Regular reflection on one's own cultural biases and assumptions is crucial. Leaders should reflect on their interactions with people from different cultures to understand their own cultural conditioning and how it affects their perceptions and behavior.

4. Seeking Feedback: Constructive feedback from peers, mentors, or team members from diverse backgrounds can provide leaders with insights into their cross-cultural

interactions. This feedback can help identify areas of strength and those requiring improvement.

5. Language Learning: While not always feasible, learning a new language can significantly boost CQ. It not only aids in communication but also provides deeper insights into the cultural nuances of the language's native speakers.

6. Building Diverse Networks: Cultivating a diverse professional network exposes leaders to a variety of perspectives and experiences. These networks can be a valuable resource for learning and understanding different cultural contexts.

7. Mentoring and Coaching: Engaging with a mentor or coach who has high CQ can provide leaders with guidance, advice, and feedback to develop their own cultural intelligence.

By developing cultural intelligence, global leaders can navigate the complexities of the multicultural business world more effectively, fostering inclusive and harmonious workplaces, and driving successful international collaborations.

Effective communication in a multicultural context requires an understanding and accommodation of cultural differences to foster mutual understanding. This involves more than just the words spoken; it's about how the message is conveyed and perceived across different cultures.

One key aspect is being aware of and sensitive to cultural communication styles. Some cultures prefer direct and straightforward communication, while others may favor a more indirect and nuanced approach. Understanding these differences helps in tailoring the communication style to suit the audience, ensuring that the message is conveyed effectively without misunderstanding or offense.

Active listening is crucial in multicultural communication. It involves attentively listening to understand the speaker's perspective, rather than just waiting to respond. This shows respect for the speaker and helps in gaining a deeper understanding of their viewpoint, which is essential for effective communication across cultures. Non-verbal cues play a significant role in communication and can vary greatly between cultures. For instance, gestures, eye contact, and body language can have different meanings in different cultural contexts. Being mindful of these non-verbal elements and how they might be interpreted can help prevent miscommunications.

Clarity and simplicity in language are important, especially when communicating with non-native speakers or in a diverse group. Avoiding jargon, slang, and idioms that may not translate well across cultures can help in ensuring that the message is clear and understood by all. Building a shared context can also aid in effective communication. This involves creating a common ground of understanding, which can be achieved by using universal examples or experiences, or by explicitly explaining concepts that might be culturally specific.

Demonstrating empathy and openness is key. Showing a genuine interest in and respect for different cultural backgrounds and perspectives fosters a sense of trust and openness, encouraging more effective and meaningful communication. Building and managing teams that are culturally diverse and geographically dispersed requires a strategic approach that acknowledges and leverages the strengths of diversity while overcoming the challenges of distance. A fundamental strategy is to establish clear and common goals. Ensuring that all team members, regardless of their location or cultural background, understand and are committed to shared objectives is crucial. This common purpose serves as a unifying force, guiding the team's efforts and fostering a sense of belonging and commitment.

Effective communication is key in managing dispersed teams. Utilizing various communication technologies such as video conferencing, instant messaging, and collaborative online tools can help bridge the geographical gap. Regular virtual meetings and check-ins can maintain team cohesion and ensure everyone is on the same page. Cultural awareness and sensitivity are essential in managing diverse teams. Leaders should foster an inclusive environment where cultural differences are respected and valued. This can be achieved through cultural competence training, encouraging open dialogue about cultural differences, and being mindful of cultural nuances in communication and decision-making.

Flexibility in work practices and schedules is important to accommodate different time zones and work styles. Allowing for flexible working hours and being considerate of the various time zones when scheduling meetings can demonstrate respect for team members' local contexts and promote a more inclusive work environment. Building trust is particularly important in dispersed teams. This involves not only trusting in the abilities and commitment of team members but also in building interpersonal trust. Creating opportunities for team members to share personal experiences and get to know each other on a more personal level can help build this trust.

Encouraging collaboration and knowledge sharing is another effective strategy. By creating opportunities for team members to work together on projects and share their expertise, leaders can foster a collaborative environment that leverages the diverse skills and perspectives of the team. Recognizing and celebrating the achievements of the team and its members can also strengthen team dynamics. Acknowledging the contributions of all team members, regardless of their location, can boost morale and reinforce a sense of unity.

Navigating Cultural Differences in Leadership

Adapting leadership styles to be effective across different cultural contexts is a critical skill in today's globalized business environment. Leaders must be versatile and agile, able to switch between leadership styles as the situation and cultural context demand. This adaptability can be achieved through adaptive and situational leadership approaches.

Adaptive Leadership

Adaptive leadership is about adjusting one's style to meet the needs of the environment and the team. In different cultural contexts, this might mean shifting from a directive style to a more collaborative one or vice versa. For example, in a culture that values hierarchy and structure, a more directive approach might be effective. In contrast, in cultures that value egalitarianism, a participative approach might be more appropriate. Adaptive leaders are adept at reading the cultural environment and adjusting their style accordingly.

Situational Leadership

Situational leadership is based on the idea that no single leadership style is best in all situations. Instead, effective leadership is contingent on various factors, including the task, the team's maturity level, and the cultural context. For instance, a new team in an unfamiliar cultural setting might require a more hands-on, coaching approach initially. As the team gains experience and confidence, the leader might shift to a more delegating style.

To adapt their styles effectively, leaders should:

1. Develop Cultural Intelligence: Gaining an understanding of different cultures, their values, communication styles, and business practices is essential. This understanding helps leaders anticipate how their actions and words might be perceived in different cultural contexts.

2. Practice Empathy: Being empathetic towards team members' cultural perspectives and backgrounds helps in building trust and rapport. Empathy allows leaders to connect with their team members on a deeper level, facilitating more effective communication and collaboration.

3. Seek Feedback: Regularly seeking feedback from team members about leadership style and approach can provide valuable insights. This feedback can be used to adjust and refine leadership approaches to better suit the team's needs and cultural context.

4. Foster an Inclusive Environment: Leaders should create an environment where all team members feel valued and respected, regardless of their cultural background. Encouraging open dialogue and ensuring that all voices are heard can help in building a more inclusive and harmonious team.

5. Be Flexible and Open-minded: Flexibility and open-mindedness are key in adapting leadership styles. Leaders should be open to new ways of working and leading, willing to learn and grow from their experiences in different cultural contexts.

By employing adaptive and situational leadership approaches, leaders can navigate the complexities of different cultural environments more effectively. This flexibility not only enhances their leadership effectiveness but also fosters a more inclusive and productive organizational culture.

Managing and resolving conflicts that arise from cultural differences is a critical skill in multicultural leadership. Understanding the underlying causes of these conflicts and employing appropriate techniques is essential for maintaining harmony and productivity within diverse teams.

One effective technique is to foster open and respectful communication. Encourage team members to openly express their concerns and viewpoints. This open dialogue can help in identifying the root causes of conflicts, which often stem from misunderstandings or misinterpretations due to cultural differences. Active listening plays a vital role in conflict resolution. Leaders should practice active listening, giving full attention to the speaker, acknowledging their points, and understanding their perspective. This approach can help de-escalate tensions and demonstrate empathy, paving the way for mutual understanding.

Educating the team about cultural differences is also important. Providing training or workshops on cultural awareness can help team members understand and appreciate each other's backgrounds and viewpoints. This knowledge can prevent conflicts from arising and aid in resolving them when they do occur.

Mediation can be a useful technique in resolving conflicts. In cases where conflicts are complex or challenging to resolve, bringing in a neutral third party to mediate can help facilitate a resolution. The mediator can help navigate the cultural nuances and ensure that all parties are heard and understood. It's also essential to create a culture of inclusivity and respect. Leaders should set the tone by modeling inclusive behavior and not tolerating any form of cultural insensitivity or discrimination. An inclusive environment can reduce the likelihood of conflicts arising from cultural misunderstandings. Another technique is to find common ground. Despite cultural differences, finding shared interests, goals, or values can help in building bridges and resolving conflicts. Focusing on these commonalities can shift the focus from differences to similarities, fostering a sense of unity and cooperation.

Being adaptable and flexible in conflict resolution strategies is crucial. Leaders should recognize that what works in one cultural context may not work in another and be prepared to adapt their approach as needed. Leveraging cultural diversity as a source of innovation and competitive advantage is an increasingly important strategy in today's global business environment. Leaders who recognize and harness the potential of their diverse teams can achieve remarkable creativity and gain a significant edge in the market.

Leaders can tap into the diverse perspectives and experiences that each team member brings to the table. Different cultural backgrounds often mean different ways of thinking and problem-solving. When these diverse perspectives are combined, they can lead to more creative and innovative solutions than homogenous groups might generate. This diversity of thought is a powerful tool in brainstorming sessions, strategy development, and problem-solving.

Encouraging collaboration among team members from diverse backgrounds can also spark innovation. Collaboration in a diverse team can lead to a synergy of ideas, where the strengths of one culture can complement the strengths of another. Leaders should create opportunities for cross-cultural teams to work together on projects, fostering an environment where everyone feels valued and encouraged to share their ideas.

Understanding and connecting with a global customer base is another area where cultural diversity can be leveraged. Teams with a wide range of cultural insights can provide valuable perspectives on how to meet the needs and preferences of different customer segments. This can lead to more effective marketing strategies, product development tailored to various markets, and improved customer satisfaction.

Leaders can also use cultural diversity to enhance organizational learning. By encouraging team members to share their unique knowledge and experiences, organizations can learn from different cultural approaches to business, management, and innovation. This can lead to continuous improvement and adaptability, keeping the organization ahead in a competitive and changing business landscape.

Promoting an inclusive and diverse organizational culture can enhance a company's reputation, making it more attractive to top talent, investors, and customers. A commitment to diversity and inclusion demonstrates a progressive, socially responsible approach to business, which can be a significant differentiator in the market. Leaders who effectively leverage cultural diversity can unlock a wealth of innovative potential, leading to enhanced creativity, a better understanding of global markets, continuous organizational learning, and an improved reputation. These benefits combine to give organizations a competitive advantage in the diverse and interconnected world of global business.

Ethical Considerations in Global Leadership

Maintaining ethical standards in global leadership is crucial, yet it presents unique challenges due to cultural variations in ethical norms. In a world where businesses operate across diverse cultures, understanding and respecting these differences while upholding a consistent ethical standard is essential for effective and responsible leadership.

Recognizing cultural variations in ethical norms is the first step in maintaining ethical standards globally. Ethical perceptions and practices can vary significantly from one culture to another. For example, practices considered as corruption in one culture might be seen as customary business etiquette in another, such as gift-giving. Global leaders must be aware of these differences and navigate them carefully to avoid ethical misunderstandings and conflicts.

Despite these cultural variations, it's imperative for leaders to uphold a core set of ethical standards that align with their organization's values and international ethical norms. This involves establishing clear ethical guidelines that are sensitive to cultural differences yet do not compromise on fundamental ethical principles like integrity, fairness, and respect.

Effective communication of these ethical standards is vital. Global leaders should ensure that their teams across different cultures clearly understand the organization's ethical policies and the reasons behind them. This might involve tailored training programs that take into account cultural nuances in ethical understanding and practice.

Leading by example is perhaps the most powerful tool in upholding ethical standards. Leaders must embody the ethical behavior they expect from their teams. By demonstrating a commitment to ethical practices in their decision-making and interactions, leaders set a tone that emphasizes the importance of ethics in the organization.

Handling ethical dilemmas in a culturally sensitive manner is also crucial. Global leaders should approach such situations with an understanding of cultural contexts, seeking solutions that respect cultural differences while maintaining ethical integrity. This often requires a delicate balancing act and sometimes difficult decision-making.

Maintaining open dialogue and providing channels for reporting unethical behavior are important practices. Employees should feel comfortable raising concerns and be assured that these concerns will be addressed responsibly and confidentially.

Building trust and implementing ethical practices in multicultural settings is a nuanced process that requires sensitivity, understanding, and consistency from leaders. Here's how leaders can navigate this complex terrain:

1. Understand Cultural Differences: Recognizing and respecting cultural differences is the first step in building trust. Leaders should educate themselves about the cultural backgrounds of their team members to understand their values, norms, and expectations. This understanding helps avoid cultural missteps and demonstrates respect for diverse perspectives.

2. Consistent Ethical Standards: Establish and communicate clear ethical standards that apply across the organization, regardless of cultural differences. These standards should align with the organization's core values and the universal principles of fairness, respect, and integrity. Ensure that these standards are communicated clearly and understood by all employees.

3. Transparent Communication: Practice open and transparent communication. Share information freely and consistently across the team, ensuring that all members, regardless of location or culture, are kept informed. Transparency in decision-making processes also builds trust and demonstrates fairness.

4. Lead by Example: Demonstrate ethical behavior in all interactions and decisions. Leaders who consistently act in an

ethical manner set a powerful example for their teams, reinforcing the importance of ethics in the workplace.

5. Foster an Inclusive Environment: Create an environment where every team member feels valued and respected. Encourage open dialogue and the sharing of different perspectives. An inclusive atmosphere where diverse viewpoints are welcomed enhances trust and cooperation.

6. Tailored Training and Development: Provide training and development programs that address ethics and cultural competence. These programs should be tailored to reflect the multicultural nature of the team and help employees understand and navigate cultural differences effectively.

7. Empower Local Leaders: In multinational organizations, empower local leaders who understand the cultural nuances of their regions. These leaders can ensure that ethical practices are implemented in a way that is culturally appropriate and respectful.

8. Provide Channels for Feedback and Reporting: Establish clear channels through which employees can report unethical behavior or raise concerns. Ensure that these channels are accessible to all team members and that issues raised are addressed promptly and fairly.

9. Regularly Review and Adapt Policies: Regularly review ethical policies and practices to ensure they remain relevant and effective in the face of changing cultural dynamics and business environments. Be open to adapting these policies as needed to better align with diverse cultural norms.

By following these guidelines, leaders can build trust and foster ethical practices in multicultural settings, creating a strong foundation for successful and harmonious international operations.

Preparing for Future Global Leadership Challenges

Emerging trends and future challenges in global leadership reflect the rapidly evolving landscape of international business and cross-cultural management. As globalization continues to connect markets and people more closely, leaders must navigate an increasingly complex and dynamic environment.

One significant emerging trend is the growing emphasis on sustainability and social responsibility. Leaders are expected to not only drive profitability but also make positive contributions to society and the environment. This shift towards more socially responsible leadership calls for a balance between economic goals and sustainable practices. Technological advancements, particularly in AI, machine learning, and big data, are also transforming global leadership. While these technologies offer tremendous opportunities for innovation and efficiency, they also present challenges in terms of skill gaps, ethical use of technology, and the potential displacement of jobs.

The rise of remote and virtual teams is another trend shaping global leadership. The COVID-19 pandemic has accelerated this shift, with leaders now managing teams that are geographically dispersed and culturally diverse. This new mode of work requires adaptations in communication, team building, and performance management. Cultural agility is becoming increasingly important as businesses expand into new markets and leaders manage more diverse teams. Leaders must be adept at navigating different cultural norms and expectations, requiring a deep understanding of various cultural contexts and the ability to adapt leadership styles accordingly.

Geopolitical tensions and economic uncertainties are also potential future challenges for global leaders. Navigating these complexities requires a keen understanding of international relations, economic trends, and the ability to make strategic decisions in uncertain environments. The growing diversity in the workforce and heightened awareness of social issues like racial and gender equality are pushing leaders to foster more inclusive and equitable workplaces. This involves not just policy changes but also a shift in organizational culture and mindset.

Emerging trends and future challenges in global leadership revolve around adapting to technological changes, managing remote and diverse teams, navigating geopolitical uncertainties, and embracing social responsibility and sustainability. Leaders who can effectively address these challenges will be well-positioned to lead their organizations successfully in the global arena.

In this chapter, we explored the multifaceted landscape of global leadership, focusing on the challenges and strategies pertinent to leading in an increasingly interconnected and culturally diverse world. A primary theme addressed was the importance of cultural intelligence (CQ) in global leadership. We discussed how understanding and respecting cultural differences is crucial for effective leadership in multicultural environments. Strategies for developing CQ, such as education, experiential learning, and reflective practices, were highlighted as essential for leaders to navigate cross-cultural interactions successfully.

Effective communication in multicultural settings was another key theme. We emphasized the need for leaders to adapt their communication styles to accommodate cultural differences and foster mutual understanding. Techniques like active listening, clarity in language, and awareness of non-verbal cues were identified as critical for effective cross-cultural communication. The chapter also delved into managing and resolving conflicts arising from cultural differences. We discussed the importance of open dialogue, empathy, and understanding different cultural perspectives as vital tools for conflict resolution in diverse teams.

Building and managing culturally diverse and geographically dispersed teams was explored, underscoring the necessity of establishing common goals, utilizing effective communication technologies, and fostering an inclusive environment. We also examined how leaders could adapt their leadership styles to be effective across different cultural contexts using adaptive and situational leadership approaches. We addressed leveraging cultural diversity as a source of innovation and competitive advantage. The chapter highlighted how diverse perspectives can lead to greater creativity and problem-solving capabilities, enhancing organizational innovation.

Maintaining ethical standards in global leadership, especially in the context of varying cultural norms, was discussed as a significant challenge. We outlined strategies for building trust and implementing ethical practices in multicultural settings, emphasizing the need for clear ethical guidelines and culturally sensitive leadership approaches. We touched upon emerging trends and potential future challenges in global leadership, including technological advancements, sustainability and social responsibility, remote team management, geopolitical tensions, and the need for inclusive leadership practices. The chapter provided a comprehensive overview of the complexities and nuances of global leadership, offering insights and strategies to help leaders effectively navigate the challenges of leading in a multicultural and rapidly changing global environment.

Transitioning from the exploration of global and multicultural leadership, we connect these concepts to the broader themes of the book: adaptability, cultural intelligence, and ethical leadership. These themes are pivotal in understanding the context of our next chapter, which delves into emerging leadership approaches.

In the upcoming chapter, we will explore how the rapidly evolving business landscape is shaping new leadership styles and strategies. This evolution is driven by the challenges and opportunities presented by technological advancements, demographic shifts, and a greater emphasis on sustainability and social responsibility. We'll examine how leaders are adapting to these changes, integrating the lessons learned from global and multicultural leadership to navigate the complexities of the modern world.

This chapter aims to provide insights into innovative leadership approaches emerging in response to these dynamic changes. By understanding these emerging trends, leaders can equip themselves with the necessary skills and perspectives to lead effectively in an increasingly interconnected and rapidly changing global environment.

9. Emerging Leadership Approaches

As we embark on Chapter 9, 'Emerging Leadership Approaches,' it's essential to first understand how leadership theories and practices have evolved over time, providing a foundation for the introduction of new approaches.

Historically, leadership theories have transitioned through various paradigms. Early theories focused heavily on the traits and behaviors of individual leaders, such as the Great Man Theory and Trait Theory, which posited that leaders are born with certain innate qualities. This perspective shifted with the advent of Behavioral Theories in the mid-20th century, which argued that leadership skills and styles could be learned and developed. Subsequently, the focus expanded to include the influence of external factors on leadership effectiveness. Contingency and Situational Leadership Theories proposed that the best leadership style depends on various situational factors, including the leader's preferred style, the capabilities and behaviors of followers, and the level of the task's complexity.

The latter part of the 20th century saw the emergence of Transformational and Transactional Leadership Theories. These theories contrasted in their approach, with transformational leadership focusing on inspiring and motivating followers to exceed expectations, while transactional leadership emphasized the importance of exchanges between leaders and followers, such as rewards for performance.

In recent years, we have seen an increasing emphasis on more inclusive and collaborative leadership models. Servant Leadership, which prioritizes the needs of the team and organization over the needs of the leader, and Distributed Leadership, which emphasizes shared leadership responsibilities within a group, reflect a more participatory and team-oriented approach.

The 21st century has brought new challenges and complexities, leading to the emergence of Adaptive Leadership, which emphasizes the ability of leaders to adapt to changing environments and tackle complex problems. Emotional Intelligence has also gained prominence, recognizing the importance of a leader's ability to understand and manage emotions to effectively lead.

As we transition to discussing new emerging approaches, it's clear that these developments are a response to a rapidly changing, globalized business environment, marked by technological advancements, cultural diversity, and evolving organizational structures. These emerging approaches focus on flexibility, collaboration, digital savviness, and an increased emphasis on ethical and sustainable leadership practices, reflecting the shifting landscape of modern leadership needs.

In recent years, several new leadership theories and approaches have emerged, reflecting the changing dynamics of the modern workplace. These approaches emphasize adaptability, inclusivity, and a holistic view of leadership. For each of these approaches we are going to define it, provide an application, benefits and limitations.

Authentic Leadership

This approach focuses on the authenticity of leaders. Authentic leaders are self-aware, genuine, mission-driven, and focused on results. They lead with their values and are known for their transparency, honesty, and ethical conduct. Authentic leadership is about building trust and genuine relationships with followers.

Application: Authentic leadership is increasingly relevant in modern organizations that value transparency and ethical practices. These leaders create trust and loyalty by being genuine and consistent in their actions and communications, fostering a culture of openness.

Benefits: This approach enhances employee engagement, fosters a positive workplace culture, and builds strong leader-follower relationships based on trust.

Limitations: The subjective nature of what is considered "authentic" can vary, and too much emphasis on authenticity might overlook the need for leaders to adapt their style to different situations.

Complexity Leadership

In an increasingly interconnected world, complexity leadership theory has gained prominence. This approach recognizes that leadership is not just about managing people but also about managing the network of relationships and interdependencies in complex adaptive systems. It emphasizes the need for leaders to foster creativity and innovation in dynamic environments.

Application: In organizations dealing with rapid change and uncertainty, complexity leadership can be particularly effective. It encourages adaptive and creative responses to complex problems and leverages the collective knowledge of the organization.

Benefits: Promotes innovation, agility, and responsiveness to change.

Limitations: Can be challenging to implement in traditionally structured organizations and may lead to ambiguity in roles and responsibilities.

Digital Leadership

As technology continues to reshape the business landscape, digital leadership has become essential. Digital leaders are not just tech-savvy; they harness the power of digital transformation to drive change, innovate, and achieve organizational goals. They are adept at using technology to enhance communication, collaboration, and productivity.

Application: Essential in organizations undergoing digital transformation, digital leaders drive change by leveraging technology for strategic advantage, improving customer experiences, and streamlining processes.

Benefits: Enhances operational efficiency, improves decision-making through data analytics, and fosters a culture of innovation.

Limitations: Requires continuous learning to keep pace with technological advancements and may overlook non-digital aspects of leadership.

Inclusive Leadership

With the growing diversity in the workforce, inclusive leadership has become more critical. Inclusive leaders actively seek out and consider diverse perspectives and ideas, promote an open and respectful work environment, and advocate for equity. They recognize the value of diverse teams in driving innovation and business success.

Application: Inclusive leadership is vital in diverse workplaces, ensuring that all team members feel valued and heard. These leaders actively work to eliminate biases and create equitable opportunities.

Benefits: Increases employee engagement, encourages diverse perspectives, and leads to better decision-making.

Limitations: Can be challenging to implement in homogenous or traditional corporate cultures and requires ongoing effort to address unconscious biases.

Agile Leadership

Originating from the principles of agile development in software, agile leadership is about adaptability, flexibility, and responsiveness. Agile leaders are able to pivot quickly in response to change, empower teams for rapid decision-making, and foster a culture of continuous improvement.

Application: Agile leadership is suitable for organizations that need to rapidly adapt to market changes. It empowers teams, encourages collaboration, and fosters a dynamic approach to problem-solving.

Benefits: Increases flexibility, accelerates product development cycles, and improves customer responsiveness.

Limitations: May lead to a lack of long-term strategic focus if too heavily focused on short-term adaptability.

Sustainable Leadership

This approach emphasizes the long-term health and sustainability of both the organization and its environment. Sustainable leaders focus on creating enduring value, considering the social, economic, and environmental impact of their decisions. They prioritize responsible stewardship and sustainable practices in their leadership.

Application: This approach is key in organizations focused on long-term viability and corporate responsibility. Sustainable leaders consider the broader impact of business decisions on society and the environment.

Benefits: Leads to responsible growth, builds brand reputation, and ensures long-term organizational health.

Limitations: Balancing economic goals with sustainable practices can be challenging, and initial implementation may require significant investment.

These emerging leadership approaches share a common theme of adapting to modern challenges – be it through authenticity, managing complexity, leveraging digital technologies, promoting inclusivity, being agile, or focusing on sustainability. They reflect a shift towards more dynamic, flexible, and responsible forms of leadership, suited to the fast-paced and diverse nature of today's global business environment. Each of these leadership theories offers distinct advantages and can be effective in different organizational contexts. However, they also come with potential drawbacks that leaders need to be aware of and manage accordingly. The best approach often involves integrating aspects of multiple leadership styles to suit the specific needs of the organization and its stakeholders.

The emerging leadership theories differ from traditional leadership models in several fundamental ways, reflecting the evolving needs and complexities of modern organizations. Traditional leadership models often emphasize a top-down, hierarchical approach, where decision-making and authority are centralized. These models typically focus on command and control, with leaders directing and employees following. In contrast, contemporary approaches like authentic, inclusive, and agile leadership emphasize a more collaborative and participative style. They focus on empowering employees, valuing their input, and fostering a more democratic work environment.

Another key difference is the response to change and complexity. Traditional models often rely on established procedures and may struggle to adapt quickly to change. In contrast, complexity leadership and agile leadership are designed for environments characterized by rapid change and uncertainty. They emphasize adaptability, flexibility, and rapid decision-making, often in a decentralized manner. Regarding technology, traditional leadership models do not inherently incorporate digital strategies. Digital leadership, however, specifically focuses on leveraging technological advancements to drive innovation and efficiency, a necessity in today's technology-driven business landscape.

Traditional models also often view leadership as a role occupied by a single individual or a small group of individuals. In contrast, newer models like distributed leadership and complexity leadership view leadership as a dynamic process that can occur at any level of an organization and involve multiple individuals.

In terms of cultural sensitivity and diversity, traditional leadership models do not typically place a strong emphasis on these aspects. However, models like inclusive leadership and multicultural leadership prioritize understanding, valuing, and leveraging cultural diversity, recognizing that diverse perspectives can lead to richer decision-making and innovation. Sustainable leadership marks a shift from the traditional focus on short-term gains and financial metrics to a broader consideration of long-term impact, sustainability, and corporate social responsibility. This approach aligns with the growing global emphasis on environmental and social governance criteria in business.

These emerging leadership theories offer more dynamic, inclusive, and adaptive approaches compared to traditional models. They reflect a shift towards valuing diversity, empowerment, agility, and ethical considerations, aligning with the evolving demands of the global business environment.

Leadership in the Digital Era

Digital leadership is a critical concept in an era increasingly dominated by digital technologies and transformation. It goes beyond mere proficiency in using technology; digital leadership involves leveraging digital advancements to reshape organizations, drive innovation, and create new business models.

What then are the core aspects of digital leadership? They are as follows:

1. Vision for Digital Transformation: Digital leaders have a clear vision of how technology can transform their organization. This vision includes not only improving existing processes but also reimagining business models and strategies through

digital means. They see beyond the immediate technological changes and understand the long-term impact of digital transformation on their industry.

2. Fostering a Digital Culture: A key aspect of digital leadership is cultivating a culture that embraces digital innovation. This involves encouraging a mindset open to experimentation and learning, where employees feel comfortable trying new technologies and potentially failing. Digital leaders champion a culture of agility and continuous improvement.

3. Strategic Use of Data: Digital leaders recognize the power of data in driving decisions and strategies. They leverage data analytics to gain insights into customer behavior, market trends, and internal processes, using this information to guide strategic decisions and personalize customer experiences.

4. Embracing Technological Innovations: Keeping abreast of emerging technologies like AI, IoT, blockchain, and cloud computing is a hallmark of digital leadership. These leaders assess and integrate new technologies where they can add value, improving efficiency, customer engagement, and competitive advantage.

5. Digital Fluency: Digital leaders possess a high level of digital fluency. They understand the potential and limitations of various technologies and can communicate effectively about technology with both technical and non-technical stakeholders.

6. Leading Digital Transformation Initiatives: They are adept at leading digital transformation initiatives, managing the complexities that come with integrating new technologies. This involves overseeing the technical aspects, managing change, and aligning the transformation with business goals.

7. Building Digital Skills Across the Organization: Digital leaders invest in building digital skills throughout their organization. They understand that a digitally savvy

workforce is crucial for the success of digital initiatives. This may involve training programs, workshops, and creating opportunities for experiential learning.

8. Ethical Considerations and Cybersecurity: With the increased reliance on digital technologies, concerns around data privacy, ethical use of AI, and cybersecurity become paramount. Digital leaders prioritize these aspects, ensuring that their organization's digital initiatives are secure and ethically sound.

Digital leadership in the modern era is about more than just adopting new technologies; it's about transforming organizations to thrive in the digital age. It requires a blend of technical know-how, strategic thinking, change management skills, and a commitment to fostering a culture of continuous innovation and learning.

Adaptive Leadership

Adaptive leadership is a concept designed to help leaders navigate complex and rapidly changing environments. This approach is particularly relevant in today's fast-paced and uncertain world, where traditional leadership models may fall short. At its core, adaptive leadership is about embracing change as a constant and viewing challenges as opportunities for growth and innovation. It requires leaders to be flexible and open to new ideas, while also being able to mobilize and motivate others to tackle tough challenges and thrive in the face of change.

One of the key aspects of adaptive leadership is the ability to discern between technical problems and adaptive challenges. Technical problems are those that can be solved with existing knowledge and procedures, whereas adaptive challenges are more complex and require new learning and innovative solutions. Adaptive leaders focus on identifying and addressing the underlying issues that drive adaptive challenges, rather than just treating the symptoms.

Adaptive leadership also involves a high degree of self-awareness and emotional intelligence. Leaders need to be aware of their own biases and limitations, as well as the impact their actions and decisions have on others. This self-awareness enables them to lead more effectively, particularly in situations that require a departure from conventional approaches.

Empowering others is a critical component of adaptive leadership. Adaptive leaders encourage creativity and experimentation among their team members. They foster a culture where people at all levels of the organization can contribute ideas and solutions, recognizing that the best responses to complex challenges often emerge from the collective intelligence of the group. Another important element of adaptive leadership is maintaining a healthy tolerance for risk and ambiguity. In rapidly changing environments, leaders often have to make decisions with incomplete information. Adaptive leaders are comfortable with this uncertainty and are skilled at making informed decisions in ambiguous situations.

Adaptive leadership also requires effective communication and the ability to articulate a compelling vision of the future. In times of change, people look to leaders for direction and reassurance. Adaptive leaders provide clarity and inspiration, helping their followers navigate through uncertainty and stay focused on the larger goals.

Enhancing adaptability in leaders involves cultivating a set of strategies and practices that enable them to respond effectively to change and uncertainty. These include developing flexibility, committing to continuous learning, and building resilience.

Flexibility is key to adaptability. Leaders need to be open to new ideas and approaches, willing to change course when necessary. This means being agile in decision-making, receptive to feedback, and ready to adjust strategies in response to new information or changing circumstances. Flexibility also involves being open to diverse perspectives and not being wedded to one way of doing things.

Continuous learning is another crucial strategy for enhancing adaptability. The business landscape is constantly evolving, with new technologies, market trends, and business models emerging all the time. Leaders must commit to ongoing personal and professional development to stay current. This could involve engaging in formal education, attending workshops and conferences, staying abreast of industry trends, and learning from other leaders and professionals.

Building resilience is essential for adaptability. Resilient leaders can withstand setbacks and challenges without becoming overwhelmed. They view difficulties as opportunities for growth and learning. Developing resilience can involve practicing self-care, maintaining a positive outlook, building supportive networks, and developing coping strategies for managing stress.

Encouraging and modeling a culture of experimentation and innovation within the organization is also important. Leaders should create an environment where taking calculated risks is encouraged, and failure is viewed as a learning opportunity. This environment fosters creativity and allows both leaders and their teams to explore new ideas and approaches without fear. Effective communication skills are vital for adaptable leaders. They need to be able to articulate their vision, inspire their teams, and communicate changes and new strategies effectively. This involves clarity in messaging, active listening, and the ability to convey complex information in an understandable manner.

Finally, fostering emotional intelligence is crucial for adaptability. Leaders with high emotional intelligence can better navigate the social complexities of their role, manage relationships, and inspire and motivate others. This involves being aware of one's emotions and those of others, managing emotions effectively, and displaying empathy and understanding in interpersonal interactions.

By developing these strategies and practices, leaders can enhance their adaptability, positioning themselves and their organizations to navigate the complexities of the modern business environment successfully.

Leading Through Uncertainty and Complexity

Leaders in uncertain and complex environments face a unique set of challenges that test their adaptability, decision-making capabilities, and resilience. These challenges require a distinctive approach to leadership.

One major challenge is dealing with ambiguity. In uncertain environments, leaders often have to make decisions with incomplete or rapidly changing information. This can be daunting as the risk of making the wrong decision is higher, and the consequences can be significant.

Another challenge is maintaining team morale and motivation. Uncertainty can lead to anxiety and stress among team members. Leaders need to find ways to keep their teams focused and motivated, despite the lack of clarity and potential fear about the future.

Navigating rapidly changing environments is also a significant challenge. In complex situations, what worked yesterday may not work today. Leaders must be able to quickly adapt their strategies and tactics in response to changing circumstances, which requires a high level of agility and flexibility.

Managing stakeholder expectations in uncertain and complex environments can be challenging. Different stakeholders may have different expectations and priorities, and balancing these while moving the organization forward can be a delicate task. Innovating in the face of uncertainty is another challenge. Leaders need to encourage creativity and innovation to adapt and thrive, but uncertainty can sometimes stifle these qualities. Creating an environment where taking calculated risks is encouraged and failure is seen as a learning opportunity is crucial.

Leaders must also deal with their own stress and uncertainty. Leading in complex and uncertain environments can be personally challenging, and maintaining one's own well-being is essential for effective leadership.

Leading in uncertain and complex environments requires a unique set of skills and attributes. Leaders must be comfortable with ambiguity, able to adapt quickly, skilled in managing diverse stakeholder expectations, and capable of fostering an environment that encourages innovation and maintains team morale. All this while managing their own stress and maintaining clarity of vision. Effectively managing and leading through complexity and uncertainty involves a combination of tools and methodologies that enable leaders to navigate these challenging environments successfully.

Scenario Planning is a valuable tool in managing uncertainty. It involves envisioning various future scenarios and developing plans to respond to each. This helps leaders prepare for different possibilities, making the organization more resilient to unforeseen events.

Agile Methodologies, originally from software development, are increasingly applied in general management. These methodologies emphasize flexibility, iterative progress, and adaptability, allowing leaders to respond quickly to change. Systems Thinking is a methodology that helps leaders understand the complex interrelationships within their organizations and the broader environment. By seeing the organization as a system, leaders can better anticipate the consequences of their actions and navigate complexity more effectively.

Mindfulness and Reflective Practices help leaders maintain clarity and focus in uncertain environments. By regularly engaging in these practices, leaders can develop greater emotional intelligence and resilience, which are crucial for leading under uncertainty.
Open Communication Channels are essential for managing uncertainty. Leaders should encourage open dialogue, share information transparently, and listen to feedback and ideas from

all levels of the organization. This fosters trust and helps leaders gather diverse perspectives, which is invaluable in complex situations.

Empowering Teams is another effective strategy. Leaders should delegate authority and encourage decision-making at lower levels. This not only speeds up response times but also leverages the collective intelligence of the team. Risk Management Techniques, such as identifying potential risks, assessing their likelihood and impact, and developing mitigation strategies, are vital. Effective risk management helps leaders minimize the negative impacts of uncertainty.

Continuous Learning and Development ensure that leaders and their teams are equipped with the latest knowledge and skills. Encouraging a culture of learning helps the organization stay adaptable and innovative.

Lastly, Building a Support Network is crucial for leaders navigating complexity and uncertainty. Having a network of peers, mentors, and advisors provides leaders with a sounding board for their ideas and challenges, offering support and guidance.

By employing these tools and methodologies, leaders can develop the agility, resilience, and strategic foresight necessary to navigate the complexities and uncertainties of the modern business environment.

Preparing for Future Challenges

Anticipating future trends in business and society is crucial for leaders to prepare and adapt their strategies accordingly. Several key trends are likely to shape the future landscape:

- Technological Advancements: The rapid pace of technological innovation, particularly in areas like artificial intelligence (AI), machine learning, the Internet of Things (IoT), and quantum computing, will continue to transform businesses. Leaders must understand the implications of these technologies and how they can be leveraged for competitive advantage.

- Sustainability and Climate Change: As the impacts of climate change become more pronounced, sustainability will move from being a choice to a business imperative. Leaders will need to incorporate sustainable practices into every aspect of their business, from supply chain management to product design and operations.

- Workforce Demographics: The aging population in many parts of the world, coupled with a younger generation with different expectations and work styles, will lead to significant shifts in workforce dynamics. Leaders will need to navigate these demographic changes, focusing on diversity, inclusivity, and adapting to the needs of a multigenerational workforce.

- Remote and Flexible Work: The COVID-19 pandemic has accelerated the trend towards remote and flexible work arrangements. Leaders will need to continue adapting to this shift, focusing on how to maintain productivity, culture, and team cohesion in a largely virtual environment.

- Globalization vs. Localization: While globalization has been a dominant trend, there is a growing shift towards localization in response to geopolitical tensions, trade wars, and the pandemic. Leaders will need to balance the benefits of global integration with the need for localized strategies to navigate this complex landscape.

- Data Privacy and Cybersecurity: As reliance on digital technologies increases, so do the risks related to data privacy and cybersecurity. Leaders must prioritize protecting their organizations and customers' data and prepare for the evolving landscape of cyber threats.

- Changing Consumer Behaviors: Rapidly evolving consumer preferences and the increasing importance of social and environmental responsibility in purchasing decisions will require leaders to be agile in adapting their products and services.

- Health and Wellbeing: The pandemic has brought employee health and wellbeing into sharp focus. Future leaders will need to consider the physical and mental health of their employees as a core part of their business strategy.

- Ethical Leadership and Social Responsibility: There is a growing expectation for businesses to act ethically and contribute positively to society. Leaders will be expected to drive not just profit but also social value.

By staying attuned to these trends, leaders can prepare their organizations to navigate future challenges and capitalize on new opportunities, ensuring long-term success in an ever-changing global landscape.

Developing future-ready leadership skills involves cultivating a range of competencies and mindsets that prepare leaders to navigate and thrive in an ever-changing landscape. Key areas of focus include adaptability, visionary thinking, and emotional intelligence. Adaptability is essential in the rapidly evolving business world. Leaders must be able to pivot and adjust their strategies in response to new challenges and opportunities. This requires a willingness to learn continuously, embrace change, and experiment with new approaches. Leaders should cultivate a mindset of flexibility and resilience, allowing them to navigate uncertainty and lead their teams through transitions effectively.

Visionary thinking is another critical skill for future-ready leaders. This involves looking beyond the immediate and envisioning what could be possible in the future. Leaders should develop the ability to anticipate trends, identify opportunities for innovation, and inspire their teams with a compelling vision. This requires a combination of creativity, strategic thinking, and the ability to connect disparate ideas into a coherent and forward-looking strategy.

Emotional intelligence (EQ) is increasingly recognized as a vital component of effective leadership. EQ involves the ability to understand and manage one's own emotions, as well as the emotions of others. Leaders with high EQ can build strong relationships, navigate complex social dynamics, and create an inclusive and motivating environment. They are adept at empathetic communication, conflict resolution, and building trust, all of which are crucial in leading diverse teams and driving organizational success.

To develop these skills, leaders can engage in various activities, such as:

1. Seeking diverse experiences that challenge their thinking and expose them to new perspectives.

2. Engaging in continuous learning, whether through formal education, workshops, reading, or other means.

3. Practicing reflective thinking to evaluate their experiences and learn from successes and failures.

4. Seeking feedback and coaching to gain insights into their leadership style and areas for improvement.

5. Cultivating mindfulness practices to enhance self-awareness and emotional regulation.

By focusing on these areas, leaders can develop the skills and mindsets needed to lead effectively in the future, characterized by adaptability, visionary thinking, and a deep understanding of themselves and others.

The chapter on emerging leadership approaches delved into several key concepts shaping the future of leadership in the modern business landscape.

Authentic Leadership emerged as a vital approach, emphasizing the need for leaders to be genuine, transparent, and true to their values. This approach fosters trust and builds more authentic connections between leaders and their teams.

Complexity Leadership was discussed as essential in today's interconnected and dynamic business environments. This approach focuses on navigating complex systems and relationships, encouraging leaders to foster innovation and adaptability in the face of change. Digital Leadership is increasingly crucial as technology continues to transform businesses. This approach centers on leveraging digital innovations to drive organizational change, enhance operational efficiency, and create new business models.

Inclusive Leadership was highlighted for its focus on valuing and leveraging diversity within teams. Inclusive leaders are adept at creating environments where diverse viewpoints are encouraged, leading to more innovative and effective decision-making.

Agile Leadership, borrowed from the principles of agile development, emphasizes adaptability, responsiveness, and collaboration. Agile leaders thrive in fast-paced environments and are skilled at leading teams through rapid changes. Sustainable Leadership was identified as a response to the growing emphasis on environmental, social, and corporate governance. Leaders adopting this approach focus on long-term sustainability and the broader impact of business decisions.

Each of these emerging leadership approaches addresses specific challenges and opportunities in the modern business world. They share a common emphasis on adaptability, ethical practice, inclusivity, and leveraging technology for organizational success. As the business environment continues to evolve, these approaches offer valuable insights and strategies for effective leadership.

Embracing these new leadership approaches is essential for preparing for future leadership challenges. As the business world becomes increasingly complex, interconnected, and dynamic, traditional leadership models may no longer suffice. The emerging approaches discussed provide a roadmap for navigating the uncertainties and opportunities of the future.

Leaders who adopt these approaches will be better equipped to handle the rapid pace of technological change, the growing importance of sustainability and social responsibility, and the challenges of leading diverse and geographically dispersed teams. They will be able to foster cultures of innovation, inclusivity, and agility, positioning their organizations to thrive in an ever-changing landscape.

Moreover, these approaches emphasize the importance of adaptability, ethical leadership, and emotional intelligence, skills that will be critical in addressing the evolving challenges of the 21st century. By embracing these new leadership paradigms, leaders can ensure they are not just reacting to changes but proactively shaping their organizations for future success.

As we prepare to enter the concluding chapter of the book, the themes discussed in the previous chapter on emerging leadership approaches form a crucial link to the overall narrative. Throughout the book, we have explored various dimensions of leadership, from the dynamics of individual and group behavior within organizations to the intricacies of leading in diverse and digital landscapes.

The concluding chapter will weave together these diverse strands, offering a cohesive synthesis of the insights and strategies discussed. We will revisit the key themes of adaptability, cultural intelligence, ethical leadership, and innovation, underscoring their interconnectedness and their collective importance in shaping effective, forward-thinking leadership.

In doing so, we will also reflect on the evolving nature of leadership in the face of global changes, technological advancements, and shifting societal expectations. The emerging leadership approaches discussed in the previous chapter will be contextualized as part of a larger evolution in leadership thought and practice, illustrating how these approaches are not just responses to current trends but are also indicative of the direction in which leadership is moving.

The concluding chapter aims to provide leaders, and those aspiring to lead, with a comprehensive understanding of the challenges and opportunities that lie ahead. It will underscore the importance of continual learning, adaptability, and an inclusive mindset in navigating the complex landscape of modern leadership. By integrating the insights from throughout the book, the final chapter will offer a forward-looking perspective, equipping readers with the tools and knowledge to lead effectively in an increasingly complex and dynamic world.

Conclusion: The Future of Leadership

Reflecting on the book's journey, we have traversed a diverse landscape of modern leadership concepts, each contributing to a comprehensive understanding of what it takes to lead effectively in today's complex world. We began by exploring the dynamics of leadership, where we delved into the traits, skills, attitudes, and knowledge essential for both leaders and followers. This set the stage for understanding leadership as a relational and interactive process, deeply embedded in the context of teams, organizations, and society.

The book then navigated through the transformative impact of COVID-19 on leadership and organizational dynamics. This unprecedented global event reshaped our understanding of motivation, leadership styles, and the essence of team dynamics, innovation, and remote work.

We delved into the intricacies of organizational culture and agile change management, emphasizing the importance of adapting culture for resilience and implementing agile strategies for managing change. This exploration underscored the necessity of agility and adaptability in today's fast-evolving business environments.

We also tackled the complex human behaviors in organizations, particularly in the context of new work realities post-COVID-19. This discussion highlighted the behavioral shifts and emerging organizational structures like decentralized and network-based models.

Leadership in diverse and flexible work modes was another key area we explored, addressing how leaders can effectively navigate and lead teams in various settings, from in-person to hybrid and fully remote environments.

The book further examined the heightened focus on diversity, equity, and inclusion in leadership, reinforcing how fostering diverse teams and inclusive leadership models is crucial in today's globalized business world. We then ventured into the realm of technology-driven leadership, discussing how advancements like data analytics and comprehensive big data systems are reshaping leadership decisions and organizational efficiency.

The penultimate chapter brought into focus global leadership in multicultural settings, using real-world case studies like Roche and Genentech to illustrate the challenges and strategies of leading in diverse cultural contexts. We examined emerging leadership approaches, highlighting how adaptability, digital literacy, sustainability, and emotional intelligence are becoming increasingly important in preparing leaders for future challenges.

Throughout this journey, the book has woven together these varied themes, presenting a rich tapestry of modern leadership. It highlights the multifaceted nature of leadership in the 21st century and provides readers with the insights and tools necessary to navigate the complexities of leading in an ever-changing world. The lessons from different chapters of the book interconnect and reinforce each other, creating a holistic view of leadership that is crucial for understanding and navigating contemporary organizational settings.

Starting with the foundational concepts of leadership traits, skills, attitudes, and knowledge, we established a baseline for what effective leadership entails. This foundation is critical as it underscores the importance of personal development and self-awareness in leadership, themes that recur throughout the book. The discussion on the impact of COVID-19 on leadership dynamics further built on this foundation, illustrating the importance of adaptability and resilience. The pandemic's challenges highlighted how essential traits like flexibility and emotional intelligence are in leading through crisis and uncertainty. This ties back to the foundational qualities of effective leaders and underscores the need for leaders to be agile in their approach. In exploring organizational culture and agile change management, the book emphasized the importance of the external environment in shaping leadership practices. This connects back to the earlier discussions on adaptability and resilience, showing how these qualities are necessary not just in leaders themselves but also in the cultures they foster within their organizations.

The focus on complex human behaviors and new work realities post-COVID-19 illustrated the importance of understanding and managing the human element in leadership. This theme is a thread that runs through the entire book, highlighting the interplay between individual leadership qualities and the broader organizational context. Leadership in diverse and flexible work modes brought to light the significance of inclusivity and cultural intelligence in modern leadership. This ties in with earlier discussions on the importance of understanding and adapting to various external factors, including cultural differences and changing work environments.

The emphasis on diversity, equity, and inclusion, as well as technology-driven leadership, further reinforced the need for leaders to be well-rounded, aware of societal shifts, and technologically savvy. These chapters highlight how contemporary leadership is not just about managing people but also about understanding and leveraging broader social and technological trends. The exploration of global leadership and emerging leadership approaches brought together all these themes, showcasing how effective leadership today requires a blend of personal qualities, adaptability to external changes, technological understanding, and a commitment to inclusivity and sustainability.

The book presents a comprehensive picture of leadership, where personal development, adaptability, understanding of the external environment, technological savvy, and a commitment to inclusivity and ethical practices all intersect. This holistic view is crucial for leaders looking to navigate the complex and rapidly evolving landscape of contemporary organizations.

The COVID-19 pandemic has had a profound impact on leadership and organizational dynamics, accelerating certain trends and shifting others in ways that will have lasting effects. One of the most significant impacts has been the acceleration of digital transformation. The pandemic forced organizations to adopt remote work technologies at an unprecedented pace. Leaders had to quickly embrace digital tools for communication, collaboration, and operations, a trend that likely would have taken years to evolve under normal circumstances. This rapid digitalization has also highlighted the need for leaders to be digitally savvy and adaptable.

The pandemic underscored the importance of agile leadership. The unpredictability and rapid changes brought about by COVID-19 required leaders to be more flexible and responsive than ever. Leaders had to make quick decisions with limited information, adjust strategies frequently, and pivot operations in response to evolving conditions. This agility will likely remain a critical component of leadership even post-pandemic.

Another trend accelerated by the pandemic is the focus on employee well-being. The health crisis brought the physical and mental well-being of employees to the forefront. Leaders had to address not just the physical safety of their teams but also their mental health as many struggled with isolation, anxiety, and burnout. This has led to a broader understanding and appreciation of the role of empathy and emotional intelligence in leadership.

The pandemic also highlighted the importance of resilience, both at the individual and organizational levels. Leaders had to navigate their own challenges while also supporting their teams and ensuring the survival and success of their organizations. Building resilience into the fabric of the organization has become a key focus, ensuring that businesses can withstand future shocks. COVID-19 has brought about a reevaluation of work models. The shift to remote work has led many organizations to reconsider the necessity of traditional office-based work. Leaders are now exploring more flexible, hybrid work models, which can have significant implications for organizational culture, collaboration, and work-life balance.

The pandemic has emphasized the need for responsible and ethical leadership. Leaders had to make difficult decisions with far-reaching consequences, balancing business continuity with the safety and well-being of employees and customers. This has reinforced the idea that leaders must consider the broader social and ethical implications of their decisions.

Looking ahead, several potential future developments in leadership are poised to shape the landscape of organizations and the role of leaders. These developments reflect the ongoing evolution of technology, work practices, and societal expectations.

Increasing Importance of AI and Machine Learning

Artificial Intelligence (AI) and machine learning are set to play an even more significant role in decision-making, strategy development, and operational efficiency. Leaders will need to understand the capabilities and limitations of these technologies, integrating them into various aspects of their business. This integration will require a balance between leveraging AI for competitive advantage and addressing ethical concerns, such as privacy and bias.

Continuous Evolution of Remote Work

The pandemic has fundamentally shifted perceptions of remote work, and this trend is likely to continue evolving. Leaders will need to adapt to a future where hybrid work models become the norm, requiring a rethinking of collaboration, communication, and company culture. This will involve finding new ways to foster engagement, maintain team cohesion, and ensure productivity in a dispersed work environment.

Growing Emphasis on Sustainability and Social Responsibility

There is a rising demand for leaders to prioritize sustainability and social responsibility. The focus will be on developing sustainable business models that consider environmental impact and contribute positively to society. Leaders will need to integrate these considerations into their core strategies, balancing profitability with social and environmental stewardship.

Focus on Inclusivity and Diversity

As the workforce becomes increasingly diverse, leaders will need to place a greater emphasis on inclusivity and diversity. This involves creating an environment where diverse perspectives are valued and leveraged for innovation. Leaders will need to develop skills in managing diverse teams and promoting equity and inclusion at all organizational levels.

Navigating Geopolitical and Economic Uncertainty

The future is likely to bring continued geopolitical and economic uncertainty. Leaders will need to be adept at navigating these complexities, making strategic decisions that account for global market dynamics and political shifts. This will require a keen understanding of international relations, economic trends, and the ability to adapt strategies accordingly.

Enhanced Focus on Employee Well-being

Employee well-being will continue to be a priority, with a growing recognition of its impact on productivity and retention. Leaders will need to focus on creating supportive work environments that prioritize mental health, work-life balance, and overall well-being.

Future developments in leadership will revolve around technological advancements, evolving work practices, and an increased focus on sustainability, social responsibility, inclusivity, and navigating uncertainty. Leaders who can adapt to these changes and harness them effectively will be well-positioned to lead their organizations successfully into the future.

As we look towards the future, the role of leaders is expected to undergo significant transformations in response to evolving organizational needs, societal expectations, and technological advancements. This evolution marks a departure from traditional leadership paradigms towards more dynamic and adaptive models.

Leaders are shifting from being primarily directive to taking on more facilitative roles. In the emerging landscape, the emphasis is on enabling and guiding teams to foster innovation and responsiveness. This approach is aligned with the trend towards decentralization, empowering employees at all levels to take initiative and drive change. Technological advancement is a major catalyst in reshaping leadership roles. Leaders must not only stay abreast of these changes but also harness them strategically to enhance organizational processes and outcomes. This requires a nuanced understanding of how technologies like AI and data analytics can be integrated into business operations while maintaining a focus on the human aspects of technology. The need for organizational agility is another factor driving the evolution of leadership roles. Leaders are required to be more adaptable, capable of swiftly responding to market changes and emerging challenges. Cultivating a culture that embraces change and thrives amidst ambiguity is becoming increasingly crucial.

Ethical leadership and a focus on sustainability are gaining prominence. Leaders are now expected to make decisions that consider their social and environmental impacts, reflecting a shift towards more responsible and sustainable business practices. Managing diverse workforces and fostering inclusivity is another area where leadership roles are evolving. Inclusivity and diversity are no longer just moral imperatives but are recognized as drivers of innovation and organizational success. Leaders play a key role in creating environments where diversity is valued and leveraged.

Nurturing and developing the next generation of leaders is crucial for the sustained success and growth of any organization. This process involves a strategic approach to identifying potential leaders and providing them with the tools, experiences, and guidance they need to grow into effective leaders. Mentorship is a key component of nurturing future leaders. Pairing emerging leaders with experienced mentors can provide them with invaluable insights, guidance, and support. Mentors can share their experiences, offer advice on navigating organizational challenges, and provide feedback. This relationship not only helps in the professional growth of the mentee but also fosters a culture of learning and knowledge sharing within the organization.

Continuous learning is essential in leadership development. The business landscape is constantly evolving, and leaders must keep up with the latest trends, technologies, and best practices. Organizations should encourage continuous learning by providing access to training programs, workshops, conferences, and online courses. This could also include opportunities for cross-functional training, allowing future leaders to gain a broader understanding of the organization.

Leadership development programs are another effective way to nurture future leaders. These programs should be designed to equip potential leaders with the necessary skills and knowledge to lead effectively. This could include training in areas such as strategic thinking, emotional intelligence, decision-making, and change management. Leadership development programs can also include practical components, such as leading a project or a team, to provide hands-on leadership experience. Exposing future leaders to different aspects of the business is also important. This could involve rotational assignments or involvement in cross-departmental projects. Such experiences allow emerging leaders to understand the organization's various functions, develop a holistic perspective, and build a network within the organization.

Encouraging a culture of feedback is essential in developing future leaders. Constructive feedback helps individuals understand their strengths and areas for improvement. Organizations should foster an environment where feedback is regularly given and received in a constructive manner. It's important to create opportunities for emerging leaders to demonstrate and hone their leadership skills. This could be through leading small teams, managing projects, or being involved in strategic planning sessions. Providing them with responsibilities and challenges helps build their confidence and competence as leaders.

Fostering diversity and inclusivity in leadership development is not just a moral imperative but a strategic necessity in today's global business environment. Diverse and inclusive leadership brings a range of perspectives, experiences, and skills to the table, driving innovation, enhancing decision-making, and reflecting the diverse makeup of the workforce and customer base. Encouraging diversity in leadership begins with a commitment to creating an equitable and inclusive environment where all individuals have the opportunity to grow and succeed. This requires intentional efforts to identify and eliminate biases in recruitment, promotion, and development processes. Organizations should ensure that their leadership development programs are accessible to individuals from a variety of backgrounds, including different races, genders, ages, cultures, and abilities.

Inclusivity also plays a crucial role in nurturing diverse leadership. This means creating an environment where different perspectives are not just accepted but valued and sought after. Inclusive leadership development involves tailoring training and mentorship programs to meet the unique needs and perspectives of diverse participants. This could include offering mentorship programs that pair leaders from underrepresented groups with experienced mentors who can provide guidance and support.

Another key aspect is providing training on diversity, equity, and inclusion for all leaders. Such training should go beyond just awareness and focus on actionable strategies for fostering an inclusive culture. Leaders should be equipped with the skills to manage diverse teams effectively, address unconscious biases, and create an environment where all team members feel valued and able to contribute fully.

Organizations should also focus on building a diverse leadership pipeline. This involves identifying high-potential individuals from diverse backgrounds early in their careers and providing them with the experiences, training, and support they need to advance into leadership roles. This could include offering leadership development programs targeted at employees from underrepresented groups, providing scholarships for leadership training, or creating internships and rotational programs to expose these employees to different areas of the business.

It is important to measure and track progress in fostering diverse and inclusive leadership. This could involve setting specific, measurable goals for diversity in leadership positions and regularly reviewing progress against these goals. By tracking metrics such as the diversity of leadership program participants and the advancement rates of employees from underrepresented groups, organizations can assess the effectiveness of their initiatives and make adjustments as needed.

As we conclude this journey through the multifaceted world of modern leadership, it's clear that the landscape of leading and managing is evolving rapidly. To current and aspiring leaders, this is your call to action: embrace the principles and strategies discussed in this book not just as guidelines, but as catalysts for transformation and growth in your leadership journey.

Step into the future of leadership with a commitment to continuous learning and adaptability. The world is changing at an unprecedented pace, and staying ahead means being open to new ideas, new technologies, and new ways of working. Cultivate a mindset of growth and embrace the opportunities that come with change. Champion diversity and inclusivity in your teams and organizations. Recognize the strength that comes from diverse perspectives and create environments where every voice is heard and valued. Your leadership can set the tone for an organizational culture that thrives on inclusivity and respect.

Prioritize sustainability and ethical decision-making in your leadership practice. As leaders, you have the power to influence not just the success of your organizations, but also the impact they have on society and the environment. Make decisions that ensure long-term sustainability and positive social impact.

Embrace digital leadership and prepare for the challenges of the digital era. Whether it's leveraging data for informed decision-making or adopting new technologies, your role as a digital-savvy leader is crucial in steering your organization through the digital landscape.

Develop your emotional intelligence and resilience. The challenges of leadership are not just strategic but also emotional and psychological. Invest in understanding yourself and others, building strong relationships, and fostering a resilient spirit. Most importantly, lead with authenticity and purpose. Be true to your values and vision, and inspire those around you with your commitment and passion. Remember, effective leadership is not just about achieving goals but also about empowering and uplifting others.

The journey of leadership is ongoing, and each of you has the potential to make a significant impact. Take these insights, apply them in your unique context, and be the leader that shapes a better future for your teams, your organizations, and society at large. The future is in your hands – lead it with courage, wisdom, and integrity.

It's clear that the essence of effective leadership transcends traditional boundaries and definitions. This book has aimed to illuminate the path for current and aspiring leaders, offering insights and strategies to navigate the complexities of today's rapidly changing world.

The vision for the future of leadership presented here is one of adaptability, inclusivity, and ethical integrity. We stand at the cusp of a new era where leaders are not just commanders but facilitators, not just decision-makers but visionaries, and not just managers but empathetic and ethical guides. The future of leadership calls for individuals who can harness diversity as a strength, leverage technology for advancement, and uphold sustainability and social responsibility as core values.

This book has emphasized that the leaders of tomorrow must be lifelong learners, continuously adapting to evolving circumstances and embracing change not as a challenge but as an opportunity for growth. They must lead with a deep understanding of the human element, recognizing that at the heart of effective leadership is the ability to connect, inspire, and empower people.

The journey of leadership is an ongoing quest for growth, understanding, and impact. As you step forward into your roles as leaders, remember that your actions, decisions, and vision have the power to shape not only the success of your organizations but also the lives of those you lead and the society in which we live. Embrace this responsibility with passion and commitment and lead the way towards a future where leadership is synonymous with positive change, innovation, and a better world for all.

As we close the pages of this book, your leadership journey – whether it has just begun or is continuing – stands before you, filled with limitless possibilities. Remember, leadership is not just a role or a title; it's a journey of continuous growth, learning, and impact. Embrace your journey with courage and curiosity. There will be challenges and uncertainties along the way, but it is through these experiences that your leadership will be defined and refined. Each obstacle is an opportunity to learn, each setback a chance to grow stronger, and each success a moment to inspire. Hold fast to the vision that leadership is about making a difference – in your organization, in your community, and in the lives of those you lead. Your actions have the power to spark change, your words the ability to inspire dreams, and your decisions the capacity to shape the future.

Stay true to your values and lead with integrity. The authenticity of your leadership will be the beacon that guides your team through times of darkness and uncertainty. In a world that is constantly changing, your ethical compass will be your most valuable asset.

Never underestimate the impact you can make. The ripples of your leadership can extend far beyond what you can see – touching lives, shaping cultures, and forging pathways to new horizons. Lead not just with your mind but also with your heart, for it is compassionate and empathetic leadership that truly transforms the world.

As you move forward, remember that you are not alone on this journey. Surround yourself with mentors, peers, and teams who challenge you, support you, and share your vision. Together, there is no limit to what you can achieve. Your leadership journey is a remarkable adventure, one that has the potential to leave a lasting legacy. Embrace it with passion, dedication, and an unwavering commitment to excellence. The future is waiting to be shaped by your vision, your actions, and your leadership. Go forth and lead with purpose, lead with impact, and make your mark on the world. The journey is yours, and it promises to be extraordinary.

References

Adler, N. J. (2008). International Dimensions of Organizational Behavior.

Argyris, C. (1993). Knowledge for Action: A Guide to Overcoming Barriers to Organizational Change.

Avolio, B. J., & Gardner, W. L. (2005). Authentic leadership development: Getting to the root of positive forms of leadership.

Bandura, A. (1977). Social Learning Theory.

Bass, B. M. (1990). Bass & Stogdill's Handbook of Leadership: Theory, Research, and Managerial Applications.

Bennis, W. (1989). On Becoming a Leader.

Blake, R. R., & Mouton, J. S. (1964). The Managerial Grid: The Key to Leadership Excellence.

Brown, B. (2018). Dare to Lead: Brave Work. Tough Conversations. Whole Hearts.

Burns, J. M. (1978). Leadership.

Carnegie, D. (1936). How to Win Friends and Influence People.

Christensen, C. M. (1997). The Innovator's Dilemma: When New Technologies Cause Great Firms to Fail.

Collins, J. (2001). Good to Great: Why Some Companies Make the Leap...And Others Don't.

Covey, S. R. (1989). The 7 Habits of Highly Effective People.

Csikszentmihalyi, M. (1990). Flow: The Psychology of Optimal Experience.

DeRue, D. S., & Myers, C. G. (2014). Leadership development: A review and agenda for future research.

Drucker, P. (2001). The Essential Drucker: The Best of Sixty Years of Peter Drucker's Essential Writings on Management.

Duckworth, A. (2016). Grit: The Power of Passion and Perseverance.

Dweck, C. S. (2006). Mindset: The New Psychology of Success.

Eagly, A. H., & Carli, L. L. (2007). Through the Labyrinth: The Truth About How Women Become Leaders.

Edmondson, A. (2019). The Fearless Organization: Creating Psychological Safety in the Workplace for Learning, Innovation, and Growth.

Fiedler, F. E. (1967). A Theory of Leadership Effectiveness.

Fisher, R., Ury, W., & Patton, B. (1991). Getting to Yes: Negotiating Agreement Without Giving In.

Follett, M. P. (1941). Dynamic Administration: The Collected Papers of Mary Parker Follett.

Friedman, T. L. (2005). The World Is Flat: A Brief History of the Twenty-first Century.

Fullan, M. (2001). Leading in a Culture of Change.

Gardner, H. (2006). Changing Minds: The Art and Science of Changing Our Own and Other People's Minds.

Gardner, J. W. (1990). On Leadership.

Gladwell, M. (2000). The Tipping Point: How Little Things Can Make a Big Difference.

Goleman, D. (1995). Emotional Intelligence.

Grant, A. (2013). Give and Take: A Revolutionary Approach to Success.

Greenleaf, R. K. (1977). Servant Leadership: A Journey into the Nature of Legitimate Power and Greatness.

Groysberg, B., & Slind, M. (2012). Talk, Inc.: How Trusted Leaders Use Conversation to Power Their Organizations.

Hackman, J. R., & Oldham, G. R. (1980). Work Redesign.

Hambrick, D. C., & Mason, P. A. (1984). Upper Echelons: The Organization as a Reflection of Its Top Managers.

Handy, C. (1993). Understanding Organizations.

Heifetz, R. A., & Laurie, D. L. (1997). The Work of Leadership.

Hersey, P., & Blanchard, K. H. (1982). Management of Organizational Behavior: Utilizing Human Resources.

Hofstede, G. (1980). Culture's Consequences: International Differences in Work-Related Values.

Ibarra, H. (2015). Act Like a Leader, Think Like a Leader.

Jick, T. D., & Peiperl, M. A. (2003). Managing Change: Cases and Concepts.

Johnson, S. (2001). Who Moved My Cheese? An Amazing Way to Deal with Change in Your Work and in Your Life.

Kahneman, D. (2011). Thinking, Fast and Slow.

Katzenbach, J. R., & Smith, D. K. (1993). The Wisdom of Teams: Creating the High-Performance Organization.

Kellerman, B. (2004). Bad Leadership: What It Is, How It Happens, Why It Matters.

Kotter, J. P. (1996). Leading Change.

Kouzes, J. M., & Posner, B. Z. (1987). The Leadership Challenge: How to Make Extraordinary Things Happen in Organizations.

Lencioni, P. (2002). The Five Dysfunctions of a Team: A Leadership Fable.

Lewin, K. (1947). Frontiers in Group Dynamics: Concept, Method and Reality in Social Science; Social Equilibria and Social Change.

Likert, R. (1961). New Patterns of Management.

Lipman-Blumen, J. (2005). The Allure of Toxic Leaders: Why We Follow Destructive Bosses and Corrupt Politicians—and How We Can Survive Them.

Maccoby, M. (2000). Understanding the Difference Between Management and Leadership.

Machiavelli, N. (1532). The Prince.

Mintzberg, H. (1989). Mintzberg on Management: Inside Our Strange World of Organizations.

Morgan, G. (1997). Images of Organization.

Northouse, P. G. (2018). Leadership: Theory and Practice.

O'Reilly, C. A., & Tushman, M. L. (2004). The Ambidextrous Organization.

Osland, J. S., Kolb, D. A., Rubin, I. M., & Turner, M. E. (2007). Organizational Behavior: An Experiential Approach.

Ouchi, W. G. (1981). Theory Z: How American Business Can Meet the Japanese Challenge.

Owen, H. (1997). Open Space Technology: A User's Guide.

Peters, T. J., & Waterman, R. H. Jr. (1982). In Search of Excellence: Lessons from America's Best-Run Companies.

Pfeffer, J. (1992). Managing with Power: Politics and Influence in Organizations.

Pink, D. H. (2009). Drive: The Surprising Truth About What Motivates Us.

Porter, M. E. (1985). Competitive Advantage: Creating and Sustaining Superior Performance.

Quinn, R. E. (1996). Deep Change: Discovering the Leader Within.

Robbins, S. P., & Judge, T. A. (2018). Organizational Behavior.

Rost, J. C. (1991). Leadership for the Twenty-First Century.

Schein, E. H. (2010). Organizational Culture and Leadership.

Schumpeter, J. A. (1942). Capitalism, Socialism, and Democracy.

Schwartz, T. (2003). The Power of Full Engagement: Managing Energy, Not Time, Is the Key to High Performance and Personal Renewal.

Senge, P. M. (1990). The Fifth Discipline: The Art & Practice of The Learning Organization.

Simon, H. A. (1947). Administrative Behavior: A Study of Decision-Making Processes in Administrative Organization.

Sinek, S. (2009). Start with Why: How Great Leaders Inspire Everyone to Take Action.

Tannenbaum, R., & Schmidt, W. H. (1958). How to Choose a Leadership Pattern.

Taylor, F. W. (1911). The Principles of Scientific Management.

Tichy, N. M., & Devanna, M. A. (1986). The Transformational Leader.

Trompenaars, F., & Hampden-Turner, C. (1997). Riding the Waves of Culture: Understanding Diversity in Global Business.

Tuckman, B. W. (1965). Developmental Sequence in Small Groups.

Tyson, T. (1998). Working with Groups.

Ulrich, D., & Smallwood, N. (2007). Developing Leadership That Lasts.

Vroom, V. H., & Yetton, P. W. (1973). Leadership and Decision-Making.

Wagner, R., & Harter, J. K. (2006). 12: The Elements of Great Managing.

Weber, M. (1947). The Theory of Social and Economic Organization.

Weick, K. E. (1995). Sensemaking in Organizations.

Welch, J., & Welch, S. (2005). Winning.

Wheatley, M. J. (1999). Leadership and the New Science: Discovering Order in a Chaotic World.

White, R. P., & Hodgson, P. (2003). Coaching Leaders: Guiding People Who Guide Others.

Yukl, G. (2006). Leadership in Organizations.

Zaleznik, A. (1977). Managers and Leaders: Are They Different?

Zenger, J. H., & Folkman, J. (2002). The Extraordinary Leader: Turning Good Managers into Great Leaders.

Zheng, W., & Gardner, W. L. (2018). Theories and Models of Leadership.

Zimbardo, P. G. (2007). The Lucifer Effect: Understanding How Good People Turn Evil.

Zook, C., & Allen, J. (2001). Profit from the Core: A Return to Growth in Turbulent Times.

Zuboff, S. (1988). In the Age of the Smart Machine: The Future of Work and Power.

Uhl-Bien, M., & Arena, M. (2018). Leadership for Organizational Adaptability: A Theoretical Synthesis and Integrative Framework.

Van Vugt, M., & Ahuja, A. (2010). Naturally Selected: The Evolutionary Science of Leadership.

Voelpel, S. C., Leibold, M., & Eckhoff, R. A. (2006). The Tyranny of the Balanced Scorecard in the Innovation Economy.

Waldman, D. A., & Siegel, D. (2008). Defining the Socially Responsible Leader.

Waterman, R. H. (1987). The Renewal Factor: How the Best Get and Keep the Competitive Edge.

Westley, F., & Mintzberg, H. (1989). Visionary Leadership and Strategic Management.

Xu, J., & Thomas, H. C. (2011). How Effective are Executive Education Programs? A Study of the Impact of Executive Education on Individual and Organizational Outcomes.

Yammarino, F. J., & Dansereau, F. (2008). Multi-Level Issues in Organizational Behavior and Leadership.

Yost, P. R., & Plunkett, M. M. (2009). Real Time Leadership Development.

Zak, P. J. (2017). Trust Factor: The Science of Creating High-Performance Companies.